Praise for *Healing Your Family History*

"Healing Your Family History is an absolutely stunning title and an idea of profound significance. Those who discover its truth and act upon it will become powerful agents of positive change in their families."

— **Stephen R. Covey,** the author of
The 7 Habits of Highly Effective People and
The 7 Habits of Highly Effective Families

"Healing Your Family History is preventive
medici   ng, and
right (read."

— Chri   thor of
Wor   and
Mother-Daughter Wisdom

*"**Healing Your Family History** is a fascinating concept with helpful tools that can have far-reaching results in healing hearts, because let's face it—we are all human, so family relationships can oftentimes be imperfect. A must-read for anyone who belongs to a family."*

— **Marie Osmond,** entertainer

"Following the correct principles beautifully illustrated in this book will result in a happier and more fulfilling life. I happily recommend this book to anyone who is serious about making significant changes in their life."

— **James Jones, Ph.D.,** the director of the
Familyhood Education Foundation and
the author of *"Let's Fix the Kids!"*

LAS VEGAS-CLARK COUNTY
LIBRARY DISTRICT
833 LAS VEGAS BLVD. N.
LAS VEGAS, NEVADA 89101

JAN 23 2007

HEALING
YOUR FAMILY
HISTORY

ALSO BY REBECCA LINDER HINTZE

It's Time to Dance: A Guide to Emotional Freedom

❧

HAY HOUSE TITLES OF RELATED INTEREST

Books

Everything You Need to Know to Feel Go(o)d,
by Candace B. Pert, Ph.D., with Nancy Marriott

If I Can Forgive, So Can You: *My Autobiography of How
I Overcame My Past and Healed My Life,* by Denise Linn

Left to Tell: *Discovering God Amidst the Rwandan Holocaust,*
by Immaculée Ilibagiza, with Steve Erwin

There's Always Help; There's Always Hope:
*An Award-Winning Psychiatrist Shows You How to Heal
Your Body, Mind, and Spirit,* by Eve A. Wood, M.D.

You Can Heal Your Life, by Louise L. Hay

Card Decks

The Language of Letting Go Cards, by Melody Beattie

Wisdom for Healing Cards, by Caroline Myss

Women's Bodies, Women's Wisdom Healing Cards,
by Christiane Northrup, M.D.

❧

Please visit Hay House USA: **www.hayhouse.com**®
Hay House Australia: **www.hayhouse.com.au**
Hay House UK: **www.hayhouse.co.uk**
Hay House South Africa: **orders@psdprom.co.za**
Hay House India: **www.hayhouseindia.co.in**

HEALING
YOUR FAMILY
HISTORY

5 STEPS TO BREAK FREE OF
DESTRUCTIVE PATTERNS

REBECCA LINDER HINTZE

HAY HOUSE, INC.
Carlsbad, California
London • Sydney • Johannesburg
Vancouver • Hong Kong • New Delhi

Copyright © 2006 by Rebecca Linder Hintze

Published and distributed in the United States by: Hay House, Inc.: www.hayhouse.com • *Published and distributed in Australia by:* Hay House Australia Pty. Ltd.: www.hayhouse.com.au • *Published and distributed in the United Kingdom by:* Hay House UK, Ltd.: www. hayhouse.co.uk • *Published and distributed in the Republic of South Africa by:* Hay House SA (Pty), Ltd.: orders@psdprom.co.za • *Distributed in Canada by:* Raincoast: www.raincoast.com • *Published in India by:* Hay House Publications (India) Pvt. Ltd.: www.hayhouseindia.co.in

Editorial supervision: Jill Kramer • *Design:* Tricia Breidenthal

All rights reserved. No part of this book may be reproduced by any mechanical, photographic, or electronic process, or in the form of a phonographic recording; nor may it be stored in a retrieval system, transmitted, or otherwise be copied for public or private use—other than for "fair use" as brief quotations embodied in articles and reviews—without prior written permission of the publisher.

The author of this book does not dispense medical advice or prescribe the use of any technique as a form of treatment for physical, emotional, or medical problems without the advice of a physician, either directly or indirectly. The intent of the author is only to offer information of a general nature to help you in your quest for emotional and spiritual well-being. In the event you use any of the information in this book for yourself, which is your constitutional right, the author and the publisher assume no responsibility for your actions.

Library of Congress Cataloging-in-Publication Data

Hintze, Rebecca Linder.
  Healing your family history : 5 steps to break free of destructive patterns / Rebecca Linder Hintze.
     p. cm.
  Includes bibliographical references.
  ISBN-13: 978-1-4019-0797-6 (tradepaper)
  ISBN-10: 1-4019-0797-0 (tradepaper)
  1. Family--Psychological aspects. 2. Self-esteem. 3. Self-help techniques. I. Title.
  HQ734.H65 2006
  158.2'4--dc22   2006002513

ISBN 13: 978-1-4019-0797-6
ISBN 10: 1-4019-0797-0

09 08 07 06   4 3 2 1
1st printing, October 2006

Printed in the United States of America

*To my eternal family—
may this message change
the past, the present,
and the course
of our future.*

CONTENTS

"The heritage of the past
is the seed that brings forth
the harvest of the future."

— Inscription on the "Heritage" statue at the
National Archives in Washington, D.C.

FOREWORD

by Stephen R. Covey

*J*ust think about the title of this book—*Healing Your Family History.* Can the present really change the past? And can it also create a new future? Talk about a paradox!

What if this were true? What if the past no longer held the present and the future hostage? Could there be anything more profound—in fact, could there be anything more remarkably motivating, exhilarating, and inspiring? What if, through deep understanding and wise actions based on that knowledge, you could not only break unhealthy cycles and prevent destructive patterns from being passed to the generations that follow, but you could also back up and impact your siblings, parents, and living grandparents?

Healing Your Family History is an absolutely stunning title, and an idea of profound significance. Those who discover its truth and act upon it will become powerful agents of positive change in their families.

Many years ago, I was on a committee of university professors, all dedicated scholars from different disciplines, who were interested in coming to understand the core principles of healing—not only for individuals, but for relationships and families as well. It was absolutely fascinating to see the synthesis of thinking, research, and writing brought together by people striving to be extremely open and receptive.

After more than two years of synergistic work, where everyone grew and learned, we ended up in a place that no one could have possibly anticipated when we began the process. The key insight we all discovered underscores the message of this book. It was that each of us has the potential to become what we called a "transition figure"—a person who can break intergenerational cycles of unhealthy habits and patterns. In so doing, we not only positively impact future generations, but also affect living people who, themselves, may have created or transmitted these very tendencies, habits, and destructive patterns. Transition individuals tap in to a level of motivation and desire that significantly transcends our own goals for personal fulfillment.

While on a sabbatical many years ago in Hawaii, I was wandering in a reflective state through the stacks in a library. I pulled from the shelves a book containing the following three sentences. They profoundly affected many aspects of my life and, particularly, my work:

Between stimulus and response, there is a space.
In that space lies our freedom and power to choose our response.
In our response lies our growth and our freedom.[1]

I reflected on those sentences again and again; I could hardly think of anything else for a period of time. I realized

that between anything that has ever happened to us in the past—such as our genetic makeup—and our current circumstances is a space in which we can choose to respond. The outcome of that can bring freedom and growth. Even though I intellectually understood this idea, the emotional force gave me both an exhilarating sense of freedom and a fearsome sense of responsibility.

Most of us have inherited genetic tendencies toward certain diseases. But we all know people who, when they became aware of such inclinations, wisely chose an action plan to avoid or at least minimize the manifestation of these illnesses in their lives. This is one illustration of the space between stimulus and response, and there are many more.

Whenever we've seen identical twins grow up in very similar circumstances but choose different life paths, we've again seen the space between stimulus and response manifest. People who have learned to reinvent themselves can likewise speak of the power in that space between stimulus and response. Our personal freedom to choose is our most wonderful blessing—well, perhaps it's the next best. Our *greatest* gift is life itself; our ability to *direct* that life is second.

Animals don't possess such endowments, and because they lack self-awareness, they can't reinvent themselves. Even though they have memory and tendencies that are cultivated by instinct and training, these creatures have no imagination to envision a different future, and no will apart from their basic psychological makeup and conditioning. Put out meat, ring the bell, and the dog will salivate—meat, bell, salivate; meat, bell, salivate. Take away the treat and ring the bell, as Pavlov's research showed, and the dog will still drool in anticipation.

Even though many animals are highly intelligent, they can't stand apart from themselves and examine their own lives; only human beings can do this. Only we can join *self-awareness* (including memory) with *imagination* (which really is greater than memory or knowledge) and *conscience* (which is the innate, divine sense of right and wrong—not just a socialized superego, as Freud would put it), and then *act independently* to re-create themselves, break destructive patterns and unhealthy cycles, and thereby become agents of positive change.

People who reinvent themselves can become models of such remarkable, inspirational power that they imbue all those with whom they become closely acquainted— particularly loved ones, including their living parents, grandparents, and siblings—with an awareness of what's truly possible.

As you study this book, I urge you to carefully follow Rebecca Hintze's five steps to breaking free of destructive patterns. You'll discover that all four of what I term the unique human endowments—self-awareness, imagination, conscience, and independent will—are required for the interior process she goes through with herself and the healing work she does with others. It's in the synergistic interaction of these four unique human endowments that you see the powerful, intuitive healing that she performs and documents.

Hopefully, you'll come away from this book realizing that your past no longer needs to hold your future hostage. As your self-awareness uncovers illusions and fears, you'll naturally feel motivated to use conscience-directed imagination and independent will in creating a new future and healing the consequences of the past. You won't change history; you'll change its effects. That's the essence of the healing process.

Foreword

Even though Rebecca and I don't use the same language regarding the four human endowments, as you study her stories, you'll notice their interplay in helping mend family histories and, ultimately, society itself. This healing must take place. A moral imperative is associated with this kind of effort, because unexpressed feelings never die; they're buried alive and come forth in uglier ways. To help our world get better, we must first address our families, which are the fundamental units of society. No civilization has ever survived their breakup.

The implications of this book for our families are enormously exciting, significant, and profound. Like a pebble thrown into a pond, the ripples of goodwill touch the other shore.

INTRODUCTION

Healing Families, Curing Ourselves

*O*nce upon a time, a young married woman began cooking a ham for dinner. As she cut off both ends and put it in a pan, her husband asked her why she did so, and she answered, "It makes it taste better." Later, however, she wondered about the process herself, so she called her mother, who'd taught her how to cook. "Why did you tell me to cut off the ends of the ham?" she asked.

Her mother said, "I'm really not sure, but I know it makes it taste better. And that's the way my mother did it."

The young woman then called her grandmother and asked again, "Why do we cut off the ends of the ham?"

Her grandmother responded, "Because it won't fit in my pan otherwise."

Have you ever wondered why you, your brother, sister, cousin, or aunt act just like Great-Grandma or Grandpa, or another close ancestor? As with the young married woman in the story, we all carry forward beliefs and behaviors learned from our forebears. Sometimes we understand them and sometimes we don't. They may have made sense in the context of other people's lives, but they don't always make sense for us. The story about the ham is a simple and funny example, but many patterns and ideas are much more complex and serious. They can have a far-reaching and tremendous impact, either positive or negative, on the outcome of many lives. For example, if two people marry and have three children, who each marry and have three children, and those grandchildren do the same, and the pattern continues for 12 generations (all marrying and bearing three children), the total number of family members descended from the original couple is approximately 3,188,643 people!

Although the young woman in the opening story believed that trimming the ends off the ham improved its flavor, that custom simply originated due to convenience. Once she realized the truth, she checked the size of her roasting pan, discovered that a whole piece of meat would fit, and changed her behavior.

We all have experiences that lead us to form conclusions about the world around us; they become "filters" through which we view the world. Ancestors pass theirs down to their descendants, who adopt them both consciously—as purposeful teachings—and subconsciously through absorption. These perceptions of reality become the basis of family belief systems over time. Of course, directives are then added and subtracted based on individual experiences. Nonetheless, assumptions can last for several generations and influence countless family members. Imagine the consequences if the learned behavior in our story wasn't cutting off the ends of a ham, but was one of thousands of unhealthy actions that mothers and fathers might pass down to their children!

Introduction

Why This Book?

As a mother, wife, daughter, therapist, and above all, a human being, I've always been driven to understand myself and discover what it might be that I'll pass on—not to mention what's been handed down to me by others. In my search to uncover the real me—the spirit self that lies beneath my generations of patterns—I've worked to expose many powerful illusions created by false family traditions. Doing so has helped me see myself clearly and thus move on to heal my own dysfunction.

To understand me, you must know about an important event in my life. At the age of 14, I contracted Reye's syndrome, a deadly disease now associated with childhood illnesses and aspirin. This nearly took my life. Because of the faith, prayers, and fasting of family and church members and friends; and because of my own will to live, my condition suddenly changed on the very day I was scheduled for brain surgery that could have left me living in a vegetative state for life. I was released from Georgetown University Medical Center within days—a true miracle. At that time, I was the only known person to have survived advanced stages of Reye's syndrome without brain damage.

Although I don't fully remember a lengthy or powerful out-of-body, life-after-death experience, I do have one short memory of standing outside my physical self. I have a clear picture in my mind of seeing myself and the monitors around me. I also recall remembering who I am as a spirit being and my life's purpose—a result of temporarily shifting out of my body.

A flood of information came to my consciousness from this near-death experience. Although leaving this earth may have seemed appealing, I know that I chose to stay. In fact, I didn't consider any other option.

Since that time, and perhaps even before then, I've had a desire to contribute to the lives of others in a significant way. To accomplish this task, I first worked diligently to uncover my true self. At times, I've thought that it might take too long, and I've panicked, fearing that I could die before getting it done. I've had my share of challenges, but peace has come to me as I've realized that all matters work themselves out in this universe.

Today, I work as a therapist and a teacher in the field of psychology. I've spent years coaching and counseling individuals about how to heal their marriages; family relationships; and pain stemming from abuse, addiction, and abandonment, including helping others identify and turn around patterns of dysfunction that are passed down through the years. My calling has helped me see that the majority of our personal struggles actually originate from our experiences with our families. It makes sense, simply because these people teach us how to think, behave, and believe. Because our perceptions are our reality, and many of our ideas are formed through experiences in our homes, healing our family's history is key to getting better ourselves.

After many years of reconciling old patterns and cracking the code of illusions blocking me and others from self-realization, I've been blessed with a beautiful life. My marriage is happy and long-lasting—and what a gift it has been to my children, my husband, and me to learn all that I've written about in this book! I pass this vital information along to you in the hopes that you, too, will experience more joy after transcending your limited family perceptions and finding the real you resting some-where within. True joy will come as you find your spirit self and use your inner knowledge to fulfill a divine and glorious purpose.

Traditions and Brick Walls

As you begin the five-step process outlined in the book, the first thing you'll be asked to do is to figure out how your family history has influenced you and what unhealthy traditions you may be currently passing on. Unlike the ends of the ham in the previous story—which were certainly being wasted but not causing any real harm—negative patterns have the potential to become great walls that block us and those we love from achieving success and happiness.

Some years ago I discovered a wall in my own family. One day after a dull weekend of housework and "honeydo" chores, I found my husband, Shane, kicking back in his La-Z-Boy chair, watching an outdoor show on television. As I wandered through the room, he made a comment about his frustrating job as an engineer and, once again, shared his secret wish to spend his life producing and hosting programs like the one he was viewing. Realizing that there might be more to his comment, I took a seat and initiated further conversation.

For six months, my dutiful husband had been negotiating a promotion at work. Actually, his goal and consequent efforts to get ahead had been under way for years, but during these prior months, he'd been promised a great new position. Yet, as the days and weeks passed, the job hadn't fully materialized.

Although he'd assumed many new responsibilities and most of the people under him knew about the promotion, his compensation didn't reflect the change. Furthermore, Shane was now performing two jobs because the tasks of his former position hadn't been reassigned.

Working hard without fair compensation and struggling to get ahead—this story wasn't just my husband's. His family history on both sides was full of people who labored long hours, tried to move up, and didn't receive adequate (let alone abundant) compensation for their efforts. Shane's experience, although it may have felt like his own, was a direct result of a pattern that continued to dictate his daily existence, along with the lives of many others. He feared that anything besides hard work—which came naturally and easily—might lead to failure.

As we sat in the living room that day, I asked my husband a question: "If you were to close your eyes and pull all the energy out of your body that keeps you from moving forward and prevents you from getting what you want, what would it look like?"

He responded, "A brick wall."

I continued, "How does the brick wall help you get what you want?"

"It doesn't."

I prompted him further: "But what if a part of you believes that it helps you. Ask that part of you this question: 'Why do I like this brick wall?'"

He opened his eyes with a look of enlightenment and said, "It helps me think outside the box. I have to work hard to get around it, so I learn more and am a more effective problem solver. It helps me do a better job than others."

I wondered, *Does it really? And if it's helping him do better than others, why is he still in the same place? How could a brick wall make him feel better about himself?* From my perspective, this was clearly an illusion. Hard work and intelligence were his inherited gifts, but I knew that there must be another way for him to direct his career and avoid the sabotage so prevalent in his family.

Introduction

I could see that this barricade needed to come down. Yet, as Shane carried on, I realized that it wasn't going to budge—at least not immediately. In fact, when I suggested that he envision it crumbling, he was unwilling to try. Instead, he maintained that the barrier was a good thing and admitted that he wasn't ready to let it go.

Wow—what a revelation! The obstacle that stood between my husband and his career goal was a wall that he wasn't willing to move.

Every family has hidden belief systems and false traditions that are passed down through the generations. We may be aware of the physical history of our ancestors; for example, we may know if we're predisposed to cancer and heart disease. But most of us don't work to discover our families' predispositions to emotional and spiritual roadblocks, which, in the end, may be as vital to our success, health, and well-being as our knowledge of medical history.

For Shane and others like him, financial success, less work and more play, and the confidence to pursue a dream can't become a reality until a false tradition is identified, challenged, and fully transcended—until that brick wall finally crumbles.

The Influential One

Unhealthy family patterns—such as willingly spending your life working hard without any compensation—can end up running your life, leaving behind powerful and long-lasting effects that you and those around you must eventually reconcile. Aristotle said, "The least initial deviation from the truth is multiplied later a thousandfold." That's why harmful tendencies become magnified as families expand. Until they're resolved or healed, they keep growing, gaining strength, and rippling outward—even if the initial problem was relatively small and happened long ago.

In a more hopeful vein, it takes just one person to affect the whole in a positive way by choosing to make a change—someone who's armed with desire, courage, determination, and a heart seeking the truth in order to find success.

A parent has the greatest potential to be that instrumental person, because Mom and Dad are the most powerful facilitators for change in families. From the moment of our conception, parents play the largest role in establishing how we feel about life, ourselves, and the world around us. They guide and direct our perceptions of our environment.

Christiane Northrup, M.D., an obstetrician-gynecologist and best-selling author, emphasizes the power of a mother's role in her book *Mother-Daughter Wisdom*. She teaches that even before birth, our mothers nurtured and cared for us: "Our cells divided and grew to the beat of her heart." Northrup explains: "Our skin, hair, heart, lungs, and bones were nourished by her blood, blood that was awash with the neurochemicals formed in response to her thoughts, beliefs, and emotions. If she was fearful, anxious, or deeply unhappy about her pregnancy, our bodies knew it. If she felt safe, happy, and fulfilled, we felt that too."[1] Our bodies still carry an emotional memory of this early experience. The entire premise of Dr. Northrup's book is that the mother-daughter relationship is pivotal, setting the stage for physical and emotional wellness throughout life.

But it's not only daughters who are affected by their mothers' ability—or lack thereof—to love and nurture. The truth is that when any child doesn't experience a caring, nurturing, and healthy relationship with his or her mother, the probability of dysfunction (such as forms of depression, addiction, and suicide) always increases.

The role of a father is equally as influential. Among other startling statistics about homes without a father are these published by the National Fatherhood Initiative:[2]

- Fatherless children are twice as likely to drop out of school as their counterparts who live with two parents.

- Seventy percent of kids living in juvenile-corrections homes were raised by a single parent.

- Children without a father's positive influence consistently score lower than average in reading and math tests.

- Three out of four teen suicides occur in single-parent homes.

- Eighty percent of the adolescents in psychiatric facilities are fatherless.

As Stephen Covey wrote in the Foreword: "To heal our world, we must heal our families." Throughout the world, the success of *one* marriage and *one* family becomes important to the whole as we work to maintain this essential unit.

Changing yourself is risky: It may create chaos in your relationships, similar to the missteps that occur when someone you're dancing with decides to change directions in the middle of a song. Depending on the nature of your partner, the remaining steps can be smooth or rocky. When you initiate a change in family patterns, you re-choreograph dance steps that your relatives have relied upon for countless generations. Initially, you—and they—may experience frustration. But eventually, as you learn and then teach new steps, they'll have the opportunity to learn, grow, and change along with you.

Dr. Northrup says, "Every woman who heals herself helps heal all the women who came before her and all those who will come after her,"[3] and the same is true for men. Any changes that you make in yourself will provide others with an opportunity for growth. I've seen individual mothers and fathers heal entire families just by changing themselves.

The quest for healing isn't limited geographically. Today, people all over the world are working overtime to heal themselves and their loved ones and overcome dysfunctional behavior. That's why Dr. Phil McGraw is so widely recognized and self-help books are so popular. Since the nature of humankind is virtually the same from one person to the next, those who desire more love, light, and truth are compelled to seek it. In the process, these individuals may become unsung heroes for generations.

Examining ourselves, our dysfunction, our family's troubles, our mistakes, and the problems that have originated because of us can be painful. But in the end, it's worth it! As our world begins to form into a story that we want to live, our joy is great enough to compensate for the pain we must endure in order to heal.

Introduction

Sally, an Unsung Hero

I worked with Sally for years, and we became close friends in the process. She grew up in an environment that was emotionally disconnected; even though her parents never considered divorce, they quietly insulted each other and seldom showed love or affection. On the surface, they appeared to be a stable, happy, and "good" family, but her parents subtly sent destructive messages to their children, which underhandedly attacked their self-worth. The grown-ups pushed the kids to look good so that they (the adults) would feel better about themselves, and the whole family lacked self-love. Consequently, Sally's real emotions weren't recognized, acknowledged, or validated throughout her childhood.

In junior high, she felt ugly and unpopular, but by high school, she began to gain the approval of older boys by projecting a sexy image. She felt that she was worthy and valuable when guys paid attention to her.

When Sally was 17, she got pregnant. Consciously, she believed that if she got married and moved out of the house, she'd be free from the home environment that had left her feeling worthless; and she thought that she'd be able to get the love she needed by having a child. Sally married her baby's father; and in a relatively short period of time, she and her husband, Ed, had six children.

The marriage had problems from the beginning, and eventually she got a divorce. Many years later, after a second and third marriage, an affair with a married man, and several sexually based and meaningless relationships, Sally decided that it was time to take a deeper look within. She'd spent her entire life feeling as though something was missing, and she was done living a life that felt out of control. That's when I met her.

After working together, we realized that Ed's critical behavior toward her and others was similar to the way her parents had treated her. In fact, all three of her husbands had been emotionally detached, critical, and unwilling to accept responsibility for their own issues—all of which she'd experienced as a child. Although Sally had blamed these men, she began to realize that the beliefs behind her pattern of divorce and abuse originated within her.

While talking with me, Sally realized that although she wanted to be married, she didn't trust anyone enough to connect honestly in a relationship. Nor did she believe that she was worthy of receiving a loving partner. Subconsciously, she felt that she needed to do everything alone and that it wasn't safe to rely on anyone else.

Further introspection led us to understand that when she was seven years old, she'd been sexually molested by an uncle. At that time, she'd tried to tell her mother about the incident, but her mom was too busy to listen, so Sally decided not to say anything for many years. When she finally did tell her family, her father didn't want to acknowledge what had happened because he didn't want to make waves. Once again, it was more important to look good than to publicly divulge this embarrassing family secret.

At the time of the abuse, Sally had subconsciously made some important decisions. She concluded that:

1. She couldn't count on anyone, not even God, to help her.

2. Something was wrong with her; otherwise, the abuse wouldn't have happened.

3. She had no control over her life (which led to the development of a victim mentality).

4. She was inadequate and didn't deserve good things.

These ideas had created, and further perpetuated, a number of negative behaviors such as a proclivity for eating disorders, infidelity, a need to rebel against authority, and misuse of her sexual energy. Sally stored anger and guilt because she felt betrayed, yet her ultimate betrayal was of herself.

She hated herself and had a distorted self-image. She'd inherited not only her parents' low self-worth, but also the desire to repress deep fears of unworthiness and mask them with an external world that looked good. She couldn't move forward without learning to love herself—not the image she'd created, but her real spirit.

When I met Sally, her kids were grown and gone from home, and all six were suffering from the consequences of their family's past. The energy of my client's problems seemed to have been magnified in the next generation. Their lives were stories of repeated divorce, drug and alcohol use, poverty, infidelity, attempted suicide, and low self-esteem.

After years of diligently focusing on herself, healing her own pain from both her family history and her own life, Sally began to rewrite her life story. She met a man who truly loves her and who's kind, gentle, loyal, and respectful. Today, she's happily married. She's also started her own business, become involved in community service, reinvolved herself in her religion, and found a greater understanding of her individual worth.

As Sally changed, I watched her kids' lives shift as well, even though her focus was mainly on herself. But her influence led her adult children to a pathway of personal healing. They were already grown when she began her journey and had formed their own philosophies of life, so some were more ready and willing to change than others. However, even those who weren't as open have been affected by the alterations that their mother made. The examples we set when we move forward always indirectly help those who are resistant simply because of the power of teaching by doing.

Sally is an unsung hero. It took a lot of courage for her to face her dysfunction after being out of touch with herself for so many years and blaming others for her troubles. To heal her own part in the creation of what she called her "nightmare life" took determination. Over time, her transformation will have a long-term effect on the well-being of her whole family.

A Word about Genetics and Emotions

Before you take the same steps that Sally did and begin the healing process yourself, it might help you to understand a little bit about the role that genetics and emotions play in your life. Until recently, most psychologists believed that every baby was born without any predisposition toward certain behaviors, thought processes, or beliefs. The environment a child was raised in was considered to be solely responsible for development, and everyone was perceived to have the same potential.

Today, as science evolves and our understanding of the mind and body expands, we're learning that genes play a

role in blueprinting our minds, too. These are some of the questions being asked by today's great scientists, who are searching to resolve the mysteries of the human mind:

- Are thought patterns passed along genetically?

- Does the body contain a cellular recollection of fractions of our ancestors' emotional memories?

- If so, does this influence our thoughts, behavior patterns, and subsequent choices?

We all know that our physical characteristics and health are genetically programmed; this is a fact. Thus, it makes sense that our genetic history may have an impact on the development of our thoughts, behaviors, and choices.

Steven Pinker, a Pulitzer-prize finalist and prominent psychology professor at Harvard University, teaches that human beings have genetically inherited much of their unique nature. This author of various renowned works, including *The Blank Slate*,[4] shows how many intellectuals have denied the existence of human nature; and his research most certainly expels any idea that we inherit an empty mind when we're born. While many scientists still embrace aspects of other theories, today most concur with Pinker that the idea of the blank slate was a myth.

Research done by Candace B. Pert, Ph.D., a former professor at Georgetown University Medical School and the author of *Molecules of Emotion*,[5] suggests that short chains of amino acids called peptides and receptors—which are tiny molecules—are the "physiological correlates of emotion." Pert's work sheds new light on the physical nature of feelings and the powerful effects that they have on our bodies. Because of her research and other relevant studies, we can consider the possibility that our emotions are passed from one generation to the next in a physical form.

Further validating the idea that our thought patterns are not only learned, but also passed on genetically, are studies done on twins separated at birth. In a number of cases, these individuals who were raised in completely different environments have grown up with much of the same emotional makeup. Twins researcher Nancy L. Segal, Ph.D., discusses this compelling research in her book *Entwined Lives: Twins and What They Tell Us about Human Behavior.*[6] In one of the many examples that she uses to support her research, she talks about identical twin brothers who were separated at birth and then reunited at the age of 39. In addition to having the same jobs, cars, hobbies, and health histories, each discovered in the other a long-lost best friend. Their thought patterns led them to create experiences so similar that it's too peculiar and hard to explain based on chance alone.

Although science hasn't yet proven theories such as those I've just discussed, no one can dispute the fact that our ancestors pass along their beliefs to us through purposeful and accidental lessons. For example, when I was 40, my husband and I decided to take our kids on a Caribbean cruise, and we invited my grandmother to go along. Up until then, I'd spent very little time with her. Throughout my childhood, she'd lived far away, and because of distance and money, we only saw each other for a couple of days every few years. I thought it would be wonderful to spend a week together and get to know her better.

As I arranged for the trip, we had many occasions to talk on the phone, speaking more during that time

than we had in a decade. As we handled the details of the vacation, I was amazed by how much we were alike. Our thought processes seemed nearly identical, as did our concerns about the fine points of traveling. Hanging in my office (where I sat to plan this event) was a picture that my grandmother had painted many years ago, which my father had given to me. Each time she and I talked, I'd hang up the phone, look at the painting, and think about her. I didn't grow up with her influence, but it was obvious to both of us that I'm her granddaughter. Considering the similarities, you'd think that she'd been a part of my everyday life.

If you've ever wondered why you not only resemble but also act just like your grandmother or grandfather, now you know: You're part of them, and they're part of you. We're tied to our heritage in a powerful way, and if we want to change our individual behavior or beliefs and heal ourselves, knowledge about our history becomes perhaps the most important data we need. In order to move forward, we must know what our forebears have passed on to us and what they've communicated to each other, both consciously and unconsciously, throughout the years.

It's All about Emotion

We also need to be willing to confront the emotions that may exist as a result of everything that's been passed down to us. Feelings have been widely overlooked in our society, and most of us have learned to block and suppress them for a few good reasons. For one, we've been taught to do so by our ancestors. For many people, it's easier to hide overwhelming sensations than to face them head-on. Other individuals find that emotions make them feel vulnerable and/or weak. For self-protection, they naturally avoid anything that causes them to feel insecure or powerless. (I should point out that just because we believe our emotions make us vulnerable doesn't mean that it's true.) Finally, negative responses—such as fear—can be misguiding.

Another reason why we suppress emotions is simply because this is the only way we know how to handle them. Most of us don't realize that it's safe to identify and embrace our worries—we fear our fears. As a result, we aren't able to effectively communicate what's going on inside of us. Rather than accepting and understanding our negative feelings, we often hide them and hope that they'll go away.

But emotions teach those who are willing to pay attention. By processing them, we learn to empathize, and love ourselves and others. In fact, understanding this aspect of our being is central to healing our family history, because it holds the most powerful energy that we use to create our lives.

If you're married or have fallen in love, you already know this. After all, did you marry your spouse or fall for your partner because you made a list of requirements and this person fulfilled all of your logical needs? Absolutely not. Perhaps the most important decision you've ever made (that is, your marriage and the creation of your family) was based on your feelings.

All of life is like this. You may attempt over and over again to accomplish a goal, but if you do so from an intellectual standpoint only, you'll rarely be successful. If, however, you become passionate about your goal, you're almost assured success.

Introduction

Since feelings have a powerful effect on the outcome of your life, becoming better acquainted with the fullness of your family's emotional makeup is key to healing your history. Instead of attempting to suppress or hide strong reactions, you'll find it far more effective to harness this power and use it to accomplish your goals. Sometimes the greatest gifts can be found in the darkest, deepest closets of the mind.

Your Spirit

As you work to understand your emotions—including those of the family members who came before you—and put together the pieces of your past that have made you who you are, your healing will begin. And as it starts, you'll likely be more motivated to change if your ambitions incorporate the direction of your inner voice, your intuition. Often referred to as your spirit, it's always there whenever you need answers.

No matter what the situation, everyone seems to instinctively know what's best for him- or herself. It doesn't matter how long it's been since you've listened to that voice, you still have the power to connect with yourself spiritually and intuitively. Whether you went to church last Sunday or haven't been in years, the spirit within you is there and available—always. You just need to choose to acknowledge it, connect, and listen.

What you hear can help you see your individual worth and contribution to the world. Each person is so important that maybe, just maybe, as you stake a claim on yourself and your past—not to mention your future—others will be motivated to do the same. In this way, you can make a lasting and meaningful difference in the world.

How to Use This Book

The mission of this book is to help you expose dysfunctional traditions that may be blocking you from clearly seeing your true identity and thus preventing you from attaining what you want most in life. Reading, absorbing, and applying this material will help you transform; and in turn, your family and relationships will change. In the coming chapters, you'll embark on a journey to becoming who you want to be. The five steps in the process are:

1. **Knowing what you need to change.** You may often exist from day to day without a real understanding of the underlying thought processes that govern your life. Taking the first step will help you identify the family beliefs and traditions that may be influencing your negative behaviors today.

2. **Overcoming judgments.** The second step will help you identify and work past the harsh judgments that you may make about yourself and others. You'll also come to understand how such criticisms only perpetuate a cycle of negative behavior.

3. **Getting past Groundhog Day.** This step will
    show you how to avoid getting stuck (as Bill
    Murray's character did in the movie *Groundhog
    Day*) while you overcome negative behavior. As
    you work through the process, you'll learn how
    to move forward to a new day and break free of
    the mistakes of the past.

4. **Finding the treasure.** The fourth part of the
    process will help you find the beauty that
    already exists within you. You'll discover how
    to do so by becoming willing to learn from
    opposition, turning your weaknesses into
    strengths, breaking free from codependent ten-
    dencies, forgiving others, and seeing people as
    God sees them.

5. **Making a spiritual connection.** In the final
    portion of the journey, you'll learn how to
    make a spiritual connection. Forging a bond
    with your spirit—the part of you that knows
    your individual worth to God—will promote
    happiness as you continue to heal yourself and
    your family.

This book is meant to be an interactive process. Each
chapter provides information that will help you gain
more understanding about yourself, your emotional
blocks, and any dysfunctional thought processes that
exist within you. At the end of every chapter is a section
called "The Process," with questions for you to answer.
To achieve powerful results from reading this book, it's
important to take the time to complete each question

before moving on. By honestly approaching these exercises, you'll experience exciting results.

Your life will change—I promise.

Chapter One

Step 1:
Awareness Is More
Than Half the Battle

1

*O*n a hot summer evening several years ago, my mother dropped by for a short visit. She arrived on my doorstep the night before I was scheduled to host a baby shower for a friend. At the time, I had four small children under the age of six, with three of them only a year apart in age. It was common for me to feel tired and a bit irritable as I scurried around a house full of dirty laundry, with toys strewn in most every corner and small fingerprints on nearly every wall. My mother walked in the door, took a look around, and asked, "How are you going to have a shower *here* tomorrow?"

That was a good question! Since I was used to getting very little sleep because of nursing babies year after year, I explained that I'd probably be up most of the night cleaning and cooking. My mom got tired just thinking about it, and she announced that she had other obligations and couldn't stay to help. Within minutes, she was gone, but the comment she made as she walked out the door lingered long after she'd left: "Don't forget those fingerprints on the coffee table."

I couldn't believe it! How did she notice those smudges in the midst of a dirty carpet, dust, toys, crying children, and a ringing phone? Her remark made me angry. Throughout the evening, I thought about what she'd said and why, and how her words had made me feel. *What was the underlying message in those few sentences? Why did they spark so much emotion within me?*

If you share my family's tradition of keeping a spotless home, you may relate to some memories from my childhood. Whenever my grandmother Frances came to visit, and while she was there—or nearly anywhere— she'd walk up the stairs bent over, picking up lint as she went. If I poured myself a glass of water and then walked away from it for more than a minute, when I returned, my glass would be in the dishwasher. If I used the sink in the bathroom, even if only to wash my hands, she'd wipe the sink with Windex or ask me to go back and clean it myself. Knowing this, is it any wonder that my mother was keenly able to locate the fingerprints on the coffee table, despite the mess around her?

A clean home and good cooking were of paramount importance to my mother, my grandmother Frances, and my great-grandmother Catherine (Grammy). I learned from them that *good* women keep their houses clean and prepare tasty food. It was, therefore, easy to assume that those who don't must be *bad*.

Did my messy living room mean that I was an awful person, that I was less than another, or not good enough? Obviously, the answer is no. But at that moment, I felt like a terrible mother, wife, and homemaker. On that hot summer night, my family tradition—a spotless house— limited me. My mother may have had good intentions, but her words left me feeling unworthy, as if I wasn't complying with an unwritten requirement.

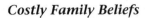

Costly Family Beliefs

All families pass along traditions. Some promote success, encourage love, and serve and heal those who choose to participate, but some customs come without anything good. (These dark, abusive, and hateful practices must be eliminated in order for a family—and even society—to heal and experience long-term joy, peace, and love.) Other habits can be a little bit of both. In my own experience, my relatives passed along both good and bad.

So is there a way to eliminate the negative and keep the positive? Absolutely. In fact, teaching readers to do so is the goal of this book, and identifying your behavioral inheritance is the goal of this chapter. As you read it, keep a pen and notebook handy so that you can jot down any ideas that occur as you learn about different possibilities and their effects. This will prepare you for the questions that follow.

Why Identify Traditions?

Why should you take the time to identify your family's beliefs or traditions? The reason is twofold:

1. Doing so will help you better understand and love others and yourself.

2. It will help you clearly focus your energy on achieving your goals.

Family traditions that hinder your ability to love, understand, and succeed are false—they stunt your ability to grow. Transcending the restrictive aspects of your heritage will increase your capacity to achieve your potential. The fact is that *all* limiting family beliefs affect individual self-esteem. This is vital information, because low self-worth is at the core of a variety of dysfunctional behaviors (such as drug abuse, alcoholism, physical and sexual abuse, and other addictions). It's crucial to expose any teachings that may destroy your sense of worthiness. Keep in mind that any information, teaching, tradition, value, or projection that leads you to dislike or hate yourself is an illusion.

Most limiting systems aren't consciously communicated. For instance, I don't ever recall my grandmother saying to me, "Becky, you'd better keep a clean house and learn to cook as well as I do, or you'll be a bad person and a failure as a wife and mother." No, she never said that. In fact, if she were living and read this book, she might disagree that she even conveyed that message. After all, she loved me and would have done just about anything to ensure my happiness. She was a wonderful, caring grandmother.

People who cherish and honor their ancestors often struggle to look objectively at their history. Respectful children and grandchildren may fear that doing so will uncover something negative, and thus degrade their good name. But discovering confining patterns doesn't mean that you're opening a can of worms or looking for something to criticize; it shows that you're willing to look at a possibly faulty process and improve it.

Letting go of the false traditions of our forebears is counsel that's been handed down for thousands of years. In the Old Testament, Ezekiel 20:18 admonishes us: "Walk ye not in the statutes of your fathers, neither observe their judgments." Jeremiah 16:19 states: "Surely our fathers have inherited lies, vanity, and things wherein there is no profit." Releasing what no longer serves you is a process worthy of undertaking.

Listen and Learn

Because many of the traditions that hold us back are passed down silently and indirectly—usually based on unspoken assumptions—they can be more difficult to define than purposefully communicated messages. For this reason, picking out family patterns may be challenging, particularly if you're fully engaged in them at the moment. But with training, you can become very good at it. The three keys to doing so are:

1. A willingness to discover the truth
2. Having honest intentions
3. Possessing the ability to listen receptively

To open your eyes, you must listen to your own thoughts, silently ponder family discussions, and pay close attention to your own conversations with relatives. Try to notice what behaviors are valued or judged, and look at the overall priorities. For instance, if your family values education, you might realize that your personal worthiness is attached to how much schooling you've completed. If wealth is important, you might see that your self-esteem is dependent upon your income.

I observed this many years ago when I was invited to join the Smith family for dinner. I was aware that the Smiths had a pattern of struggling financially, and I knew that some of them wanted to make more money. After dinner, I overheard an interesting conversation. Several of the women began talking about doctors they knew and how unfair it was that those professionals earned so much. Mary Smith noted that a particular physician she knew worked only three days a week and was very wealthy. She maintained her judgment that it was unfair and implied that this man was "bad" because of the financial success he'd attained without working long hours—or so she assumed.

Listening to this discussion helped me understand an important and limiting Smith family belief. The subconscious message they were sending was something like this: "You have to work hard to have money, and you're a better person if you struggle to make ends meet. People who have lots of money are bad."

Is there any question why members of this family had trouble getting ahead financially? As a clan, they valued hard work but not financial independence. They also didn't make playtime, vacations, or leisure activities a priority. Consequently, they all worked hard, played little, and scrambled to make ends meet.

This tradition is an example of one that will prevent you from loving others and yourself—and these are the ones you should focus on discovering. You see, the Smiths struggled to love and feel comfortable around people with higher incomes, and their beliefs about money set them up to mudsling. In all likelihood, their judgment of the wealthy doctor was unfounded. Physicians, and others with higher salaries, are often hard workers who pay a heavy price to create success in their profession.

Other customs that are worth examining are the ones that prevent you from getting what you want in life. Many members of the Smith family wanted to create financial freedom and more time to play. Under their rules, however, such an opportunity would violate the unspoken law: Don't make money or you'll be bad. Everyone would be highly uncomfortable with one of their relatives living the way that doctors do.

When your family sends you messages that are roadblocks to your goals, you may become conflicted: part of you wanting one thing, and part of you wanting another. Since your family typically provides a powerful sense of stability and much of the love you feel you need to survive, breaking the unspoken commandments may seem scary. For this reason, many people feel stuck. You probably want and need to be accepted as part of the group, even if its traditions make you miserable.

When family beliefs lead you to judge someone or something as bad, another conflict appears: Your conclusions and reality get out of sync. The Smith family judged physicians harshly, so it would be difficult for any of them to adopt a similar lifestyle—even if they had the means to do so and would be happier that way. This is parallel to my condemnation of myself when my home didn't meet my family's standards. Until I healed my self-judgment, it was hard for me to let my house be dirty without an emotional consequence. And as any mother knows, cleaning a home with children in it is like shoveling snow in a blizzard. I would have been an emotional mess if I hadn't dealt with this faulty core belief, and my anxiety could have caused undue stress for my children.

Discovering Your Family Patterns

Many silent codes are subconsciously transmitted throughout our society. Following are some common misconceptions that I've encountered as I've helped my clients (and myself) eliminate destructive family cycles. Although this list is divided into sections, most of these aren't exclusive to a single category and may ultimately affect many aspects of a person's life. Consider whether any of these resonate with your family experience, and if so, jot them down.

Family Beliefs Affecting Finances

- I must have a lot of money to be classified as successful.

- I must work hard to have money, or else I don't deserve to have it.

- I'm a better person if I work hard and do without.

- If I have too much money, I'll be prideful, and God will punish me by taking it all away.

- It's better to go without, because having too much means I'll be wasteful and greedy.

- I'm better if I'm poor rather than rich. Rich people are bad.

- I'm better if I'm rich rather than poor. Poor people are bad.

- God will love me more if I struggle, give up everything I have for others, and save nothing for myself.

- I must give everything I have to others and keep nothing for myself.

- I must hold on to all my money or it will go away.

- There's not enough in this universe. I must fight to get my portion.

- I must conserve and be thrifty because there isn't enough for everyone.

- If I have enough, others will be doing without.

- I don't deserve to have what I want.

Family Beliefs Affecting Health and Physical Well-being

- People who are sick are weak or bad.

- People who are sick are good. (It's best to have the worst case of a disease, or to be ill enough to need hospital care.)

- I must be athletic in order to have value in my family or the world.

- I must be thin to be good enough.

- I must be heavier to be good enough— thin people are bad.

- I must look young to have value.

- I'm better if I'm older and wiser. It's good to appear older.

- It's bad to be pretty. Good-looking people aren't as smart and capable as me. Or, bad things happen to pretty girls (or boys).

- I must be attractive or I'm not good enough.

Family Beliefs Affecting Education and/or Career

- I must be educated by a respectable school and have a degree to have value.

- My education or professional status matters and indicates that I'm better than others.

- I'm better when I'm in charge of others.

- I'm better when I'm not in charge of others.

- Leaders have political agendas and are bad.

- I can't trust others to support me.

- I'll always be taken advantage of in the world.

- It's good if I'm not successful. It's bad to get ahead.

Family Beliefs Affecting Spirituality

- God will love me more if I struggle, give up all I have for others, and save nothing for myself.

- Those who don't go to church are bad (or, those who don't go to *my* church are bad).

- God won't love me if I make a mistake; in fact, He'll punish me.

- People who believe in God and go to church are not as aware/smart as I am.

- God doesn't exist.

- I must be afraid of God or He'll punish me.

- God loves ____ people more than ____ people.

- I'm not important to God.

- I'm more important to God than others.

- If I go to church, I'll be good enough.

- It's good to be unhappy.

Family Beliefs Affecting Relationships

- It's better to do everything myself, because if others help me, it shows that I'm weak and not capable.

- Women are less valuable than men, or men are less valuable than women.

- Men are better than women, or women are better than men.

- Men can't be trusted, or women can't be trusted.

- People of a certain race are superior.

- I must be on time to events. If I'm tardy, I'm bad.

- I must keep my house clean or else I'm not good enough.

- The needs of others are more important than my own.

- Relationships hurt, so I'm better off alone.

- Marriage is bad.

- Love is painful. (This is common in families with a history of abuse.)

Look to the Stars

A vital gift that we give ourselves is the ability to understand and accept the power we hold to create our own experiences. Becoming aware of the many messages that influence our behavior allows each of us the freedom to step out of our present-time challenges and move forward. For example, members of the Smith family have the ability to create a new financial reality if they're willing to recognize their patterns and change them. When they're willing to see the truth and alter their beliefs, they can create new opportunities for themselves and their descendants. Until then, they may feel as if they're victims in a world they can't control, trying to make more money but barely getting by.

All of us are like the Smiths in one way or another. We have family or societal assumptions that prevent us from realizing our full potential. Thus, we have a reason to look further into our consciousness for misconceptions that may be holding back our families and ourselves.

Becoming conscious is the process of bringing into focus the underlying thoughts, motives, and intentions that govern our behavior. Harville Hendrix, Ph.D., psychologist and author of *Getting the Love You Want*,[1] shares the following analogy, which can help us understand our consciousness: We say that the stars come out at night because we can't see them in the daytime. But, truthfully, they're there all the time. Likewise, we underestimate the total number of heavenly bodies that exist in our view. We look up at the sky, see a few, and think that's all there is.

When we go far away from the city lights, we see a sky full of stars, and we're excited about the brilliant view. However, when we study astronomy, we learn the truth—that what we see on a clear, moonless night in the country is only a fraction of the stars in the entire universe, and many of the points of light that we see are, in fact, galaxies.

Our unconscious minds are much the same. Most of us are trained to look at our subconscious in a way that's similar to our front-porch observations of the universe—only recognizing a few stars in a sky full of celestial bodies. But in fact, the methodical, rational thoughts that run through our heads are only a fine covering over the unconscious mind, which is active, functioning, and guiding us at all times. As we work to create something new, we must understand that there's much more to our consciousness, just as there's much more to our universe than meets the eye. Family patterns are accountable for the majority of our awareness. Thus, understanding these powerful bits of information stored deeply within us is the first step to creating something new.

Laurine's Stars

Years ago, I worked with a woman named Laurine. She was born in the 1930s, when few individuals acknowledged the existence of the subconscious mind. Although she was a spiritually progressed woman who was highly intuitive and very aware of others' thoughts

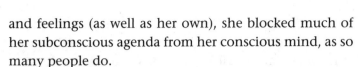

and feelings (as well as her own), she blocked much of her subconscious agenda from her conscious mind, as so many people do.

In one session, Laurine revealed from deep within some powerful beliefs. Her family's code included thoughts such as: *You're only good enough if you do everything perfectly* (perfectionism); *you must be educated and have lots of money to be good enough; others must respect you (and that will happen when you're educated, wealthy, attractive, and/or perfect); it's very important what others think of you;* and *you must look good to the world.* Additionally, they had a conflicting belief that you mustn't look *too* good or others won't accept you.

Intuitively, Laurine was aware of these unspoken rules, and further self-examination helped her realize that they'd made it impossible for her to ever love herself. They'd prompted her to believe that she'd never be able to be good enough for her family and herself. If she couldn't feel worthy, how could she love and accept herself? And if she couldn't do that, how could she care for others? Consequently, she'd become judgmental, and her relationships reflected her negativity.

Laurine had unconsciously accepted her family's laws for most of her life, although they'd forced her and other members into a pattern of being dishonest. After all, how could she be frank about her mistakes if she always had to be perfect? Rather than seeing herself for who she was (and others for themselves), she'd taken up pretending that she and her world were flawless. She had, until our sessions, avoided self-examination in order to keep from facing the truth.

In fact, if you'd asked her about her life prior to our sessions, she would have recalled a past without any blemishes. Yet Laurine had experienced abandonment in her marriage, serious health issues, a weight problem, financial hardship, lack of companionship, and more. When she began sessions with me, her dysfunction was apparent in subconscious patterns that produced unhealthy results.

After working with her, it became clear to me that most of her problems originated in her family's limiting patterns. Although she had her own troubles, her relatives' unconscious requirements for measuring up and being accepted complicated her life and influenced her belief that living on this earth wasn't positive.

Until she became aware of her subconscious programming—that is, saw a fuller picture of the stars in her universe—she remained a victim with little ability to alter her reality. As she began realizing all of this, she was able to piece together the events of her past with greater understanding, and that empowered her to create a new reality.

Laurine isn't alone; we all resemble her when our issues are created or worsened by negative misconceptions in the unconscious family rule book. Sometimes, realization and self-awareness are more than half the battle. In fact, many times we only need to recognize the illusion in order to change.

Cleaning the Hard Drive

Everything we experience in life is recorded by our body/mind. As if we were computers with complex processing systems and deeply embedded hard drives, our bodies and minds contain all the facets of our individual perceptions, including acceptance of our families' rule books. Some people can change their body/mind computer daily as new data is input, and outdated information is overwritten. Other people may rarely change, rerunning old stories over and over again.

When you lock your family's perceptions into your body/mind computer, your system begins to filter your experiences through the perceptions you've stored. Deciding that you're unworthy or not good enough because of negative filters begins a cycle of repetition, and you begin to see all circumstances through a tainted lens, blocking out other views of reality that may exist simultaneously.

Here's a visual example of this concept: When you buy a new car, you become familiar with that model and color, and from that point on, you start seeing lots of other vehicles like yours. You may never have noticed them before, but after your purchase, and even after you sell the car, you still pick out its color and body type on the road. So it is with each of us: When we have experiences that lead us to make decisions about our lives or ourselves, we unconsciously venture into the world and notice all other experiences that validate what we believe to be true.

When our brains cling to a perception, we'll attempt to re-create similar circumstances or feelings to validate it. Knowing this, it's easy to understand how families who hold certain ideas find it difficult to see beyond their own situation (that is, see other cars on the road). For instance, the Smiths can't imagine themselves experiencing life without hard work and financial struggle. They don't know how fiscal freedom feels, and they have no comprehension of other lifestyles. They've functioned with their family's beliefs for so long that they can't see other realities. For example, if they've always owned a blue Pontiac, consequently they never notice the gold Mercedes—so they don't know that they can have a gold Mercedes if they choose to change.

A friend of mine named Marilyn also had a number of limiting family beliefs and fears about money. She believed that there wasn't enough in the universe for everyone to have what they desired. She felt that she didn't deserve to have what she wanted, and if she got it somehow, then it wouldn't last. She also believed that everyone else had to achieve success before she could.

These fears and misconceptions were a direct result of her parents' beliefs about these subjects, and her position in her family. As the oldest child, she was taught to put her needs aside for those of others. That can be positive, and it had been useful throughout much of her life. It turned negative, however, when she decided deep down that her needs weren't important—and, she concluded, that must mean that *she* wasn't important. Both Marilyn's mom and dad were also oldest children raised by kind, service-oriented people. Her parents may have decided something similar in their youth and thus passed their fears of unimportance along to their firstborn. Again, putting your own needs aside at times is a positive trait, but in this family, fear rested underneath it, which fed patterns of unworthiness.

Both of Marilyn's parents worried about not having enough. In their efforts to be kind and generous to others, they struggled to keep a piece of the pie for themselves. Although they halfheartedly believed that they deserved to have what they wanted, they also feared that there would never be enough, simply because they were subconsciously afraid that they were unimportant.

Until my friend was willing to identify and change the data stored in her hard drive (her misperceptions), her reality was influenced by her family's habits. It seemed that there was never enough for her even though others appeared to get what they wanted. She was always the low person on the totem pole. That's probably how she felt as a child, and her early self-image lived on and on. Marilyn's tainted view of the world left her identifying only the times when she was left out, dropped off without a buck, and, she believed, never important enough to have her needs met. She struggled to notice the times when she might have been first, had an extra $20 when she needed it, actually bought the home she was praying for, and so forth.

Gaining Power by Changing Our Perceptions

Albert Einstein once stated: "The significant problems we face cannot be solved by the same level of thinking we were at when we created them." It is not until we understand our limited thinking that we can choose to alter it and ourselves.

I've had many clients make dramatic changes in their lives after simply opening themselves up to more possibilities. For example, a man once came into my office wanting to work through the barriers that had prevented him from creating a way to purchase a new home. He lived in an expensive area and couldn't seem to qualify for a loan. After just one session, he became aware of ways that he'd sabotaged his finances, and thus his ability to achieve his goal. Within three months of changing his perception, my client purchased a new house.

When we can see new options, we can create them. But in order to get to that point, we must change the level of thinking we were at when we created our original opinions.

Handling the Emotions That Come from Limiting Beliefs

Many emotions naturally arise as a result of our core beliefs. For example, a woman who thinks she must have a clean home in order to be a good person may become upset when others make messes around her. Her anger arises because the actions of others directly challenged her self-worth, which depends on adherence to her family's core beliefs. Another woman, who believes she must be thin in order to be valued, may become agitated when others question her weight, or observe what she eats or if and when she exercises. When our self-worth is on the line, it becomes increasingly difficult to create happy and positive circumstances for ourselves.

Feeling, acknowledging, and understanding our emotions can help us scan our core beliefs and purge our "hard drives" of undesirable data. It's important to acknowledge our feelings rather than repress them. Overcoming negative ones can help us progress in such a way that we're able to see and thus create new possibilities for ourselves.

Unfortunately, this can be very hard to do if we're emotionally disconnected. Many people in our society struggle to identify how they feel because they were taught in their homes to fear emotion. Evidence of this unconscious pressure to withhold is observed when we hear parents say to their children, "Quit crying. You don't need to fuss about that," or when we hear adults judge or criticize others who show sensitivity.

Our emotions are powerful indicators of what is going on inside of us. Further, they're part of our body's exquisite system for processing our daily experiences. Crying isn't a negative thing; sometimes it can relieve stress and leave us feeling tranquil. There may be times when we need to pull ourselves together and deal with our troubles quickly, but there are many more occasions when we can benefit from exploring and learning. When we repeatedly experience certain feelings and scenarios, that's the time to take note of what's going on inside.

When we understand that our emotions are clues to our core beliefs, we're usually more willing to pay attention to them. They can provide the information necessary to change our perceptions and eventually see new possibilities (that is, notice other cars on the road).

To reiterate, limiting family beliefs affect individual self-esteem and feelings of self-worth. Whenever these patterns challenge the positive way you feel about yourself, the negative emotions you naturally experience give you vital information. If you're suffering from any of the following dysfunctional behaviors, it's time to examine your subconscious and uncover the patterns and beliefs that are destroying your hard drive:

- Food, sex, drug, or alcohol addictions
- Relationship failures
- Abuse of any kind
- Religious frustration and/or anger
- Emotional detachment

As mentioned earlier, any information, teaching, tradition, value, or projection that leads us to dislike or hate ourselves is a form of illusion. We're all glorious, spiritual beings with divine potential. Sometimes, as we heal, we may find that we dislike our behavior (our choices), but facing the truth will lead us to uncover something good within us, not something bad.

If you feel emotionally overwhelmed, put your negative emotions to work for you. Let them help you cleanse your body/mind computer of bad data—that is, beliefs that prevent you from loving and accepting yourself.

Searching Within—the Process Begins

In order to heal the external world, we must begin within. Reality is always a reflection of what's on the inside. It's a law: As we sow, so shall we reap; what we put out comes back to us hundredfold. For this reason, this chapter and those that follow it contain questions that will help you begin the healing process.

As you respond to the questions, please be honest with yourself. Your willingness to explore the truth will give you the power to change your life for the better and love yourself. It's difficult for the conscious mind to choose to see the truth (that is, to see more stars in the sky) if your answers lead you to hate, judge, or blame others or yourself. Such negative behavior only indicates a need for further introspection.

Healing requires compassion and honesty without blame. As you're prompted to look at your family patterns—which probably didn't originate with you—it's important to feel compassion for your relatives, who may have experienced hardships because of limiting ideas. Blame is the unhealthy process of taking the focus off yourself and placing it elsewhere, and you'll feel like a victim if you don't hold yourself accountable for your decision to comply with your family's unconscious rule book. The only way to heal your current dysfunction is with full accountability, love, and compassion for your family members and yourself.

Exploring within your consciousness is exciting and gives you the power to change, so enjoy this time of soul-searching, and nurture yourself as you heal. A healthy diet, good sleep habits, and an appropriate exercise routine will help keep you balanced and make the transition a smooth one.

Answering the questions for each step in this book means that you're ready to change. Keep track of your responses from each chapter; you'll need to record them in a notebook or a journal (or on the Notes pages at the end of this book) to complete this process in full. If at any time you think you need to stop, feel free to put this book down and take a day to ponder. Then come back and pick up where you left off. Be willing to see the truth, and as you do so, you'll be blessed.

The Process

1. What is it that you want most in your life right
    now? You may write down something such as: *I
    want to make more money; I want a better relation-
    ship with my partner; I want a better job; I want to
    feel happy;* or *I want to create more peace at home.*

2. Is what you want different from what your par-
    ents or other ancestors experienced? Examine
    their beliefs, and be observant and objective.
    You may immediately begin to recognize pat-
    terns that prevent you from getting what you
    want. If so, make a note of them.

3. Do you feel that your mom and dad love (or,
    if deceased, *loved*) themselves fully? If not,
    continue with Question 4. If yes, ask yourself
    if you're willing to be honest about your per-
    ception of your family and then continue with
    Question 4. Remember, we live in a universe
    where what's naturally beautiful is also imper-
    fect. Loving ourselves perfectly is something
    that many work toward in this life; however,
    achieving it here in our human state is unlikely
    and unnatural.

4. Write down one or more traditions that you
    learned from your mother that prevent you
    from feeling good about yourself. Refer to the
    list provided earlier in this chapter if you need
    help. For example, if your goal is to make more
    money, you'll want to look at her beliefs about

this issue. Ask yourself questions such as: *Did my mom feel she deserved to have money? Did she fear there'd never be enough? Was she a victim?* If your goal is to improve your relationship with your partner, you'll want to look at your mom's relationship with her partner(s). Did she have a pattern of being a victim? If so, why? Was she trusting or suspicious? How might she have contributed to problems in her relationships?

5. Write down one or more traditions that you learned from your father that prevent you from feeling good about yourself. Again, use the list in this chapter to help you if necessary. For example, if your goal is to get a better job, you might ask yourself questions such as: *Was my father content in his job? Did he believe that he deserved to be happy while he worked? Did he use his career as an opportunity to pursue a passion or to complete his life's purpose? If not, why?* The traditions you've recorded in this step and the previous one are the beginning of your list of false family beliefs.

6. Answer this question: *In what ways am I like my parents and unwilling to recognize it?* This is a time to be very honest with yourself. If you can't see how you resemble your mom and dad, ask someone who loves and supports you for help. Let this person know that you really want to see the truth, and then ask if he or she would help you identify the ways in which you behave or think in ways that are similar to your parents.

7. Reviewing the beliefs that belong to both you and your parents, identify those that prevent you from getting what you want most in your life right now.

8. Since our environment also plays an important role in how we feel about ourselves, take a minute to record one or more beliefs that you've learned from society (or from your regional culture) that prevent you from feeling good about yourself.

9. Identify which of these cultural beliefs prevent you from getting what you want right now.

Congratulations! You've completed the first step on this path and are ready to move on to learning how to overcome judgments and fears.

Chapter Two

Step 2:
Overcoming
Judgments and Fears

2

$\mathcal{T}$he world is filled with beliefs that are based on false information: Things aren't always what they seem. My husband likes to tell a story about a woman who froze to death in the back of a freight train because she believed that the temperature was below freezing, but in truth, it wasn't that cold at all. I hear this tale often, since my husband thinks it's ridiculous that I'm always cold. He jokingly tells our kids that one day I'll be just like that woman, found frozen to death when it's 50 degrees outside!

All kidding aside, the story is a great example of how potent our perceptions can be, and how they can overpower reality in many situations. These misperceptions—and the judgments we make because of them—are the focus of this chapter. Earlier, you identified the false traditions that may be holding you back; now it's time to figure out how these customs came to be. You'll begin to discover why you believe the things you do and learn how to overcome the instinct to judge those who don't agree—or to view yourself too harshly when you don't comply with your family's or society's expectations.

Looking to the Past

As you work to overcome the desire to make unjust judgments, it's helpful to take a look at the things you're afraid of. After all, many perceptions are based solely on fear. For example, it's possible that the frozen woman's terror of frigid temperatures kept her from realizing the truth: that it wasn't as cold as she thought.

We all have fears, and as human beings, we naturally make judgments—whether fair or unfair—about the things we dread. These negative assessments have the potential to prevent us from seeing some situations clearly. For example, when we encounter difficult times, we may worry that our circumstances are a result of something that's wrong with us. This is often the result of childhood trauma: Our reactions to those events wind up distorting our current perceptions, even if the incident happened long ago. And although our adult selves may know better, the child within often suspects that we're to blame for things that we really couldn't control, such as divorce, abuse, accidents, death, or even financial distress. This bygone distress—and the beliefs that we created because of it—have the potential to govern the future if we don't choose to own our lives.

A look into the past, therefore, can be very helpful as you sort out your perceptions of reality. As you review your family's history, you can uncover the distortions and judgments that you've formed, as well as the fears that created them. And although you can't change what happened, you *can* alter how you feel about it. More important, you can shift the course of the future for yourself and those who will follow.

Faulty perceptions, anxiety, and critical judgments (such as believing that you're not a good mother if your house isn't always spotless or feeling that so-and-so down the street isn't successful because he never went to college or worked as hard as you did) form for a variety of reasons. A primary cause may be the expectations you set for yourself and those that have been passed down by family members.

Evaluating Your Expectations

Many varying beliefs pervade our families and affect our lives, world, sense of self-worth, and ability to give and receive love in our relationships with one another. Some people believe it's good to be friendly, while others teach that it's best to be reserved or quiet. Some think that the only way to live is to coexist with your extended family throughout life; others believe that it's not normal to live with your relatives. Different groups may hold that it's better to be black than white, or Christian than Jewish, or European than American.

One of my favorite children's stories is *If Only I Had a Green Nose*[1] by Max Lucado. In this story, the pervading belief in the community is that you must follow the latest trend in order to fit in and be loved—even if the fad says it's cool to have a green nose. In fact, following along is the overriding expectation for members of this group. If you lived there and didn't have a green nose, it's obvious that you wouldn't fit in—and we all know what happens to your sense of self-worth when you don't quite fit in with the rest of the crowd. In truth, any pervasive belief (whether it dictates kindness or demands that your nose be green) affects our self-image and our ability to love.

You see, as human beings, we have the innate desire to be loved and accepted by others. This can bring out the best and worst in all of us. For example, when we comply with any set of positive rules or worthy expectations—whether they're explicitly laid out or unintentionally communicated by those we care for—we have the benefit of feeling as if we fit in; we feel loved and valued. This usually makes us happy, which tends to help us do and be our best.

But when we can't live up to all the expectations that surround us—or if they're unrealistic and unfair—most of us feel bad (even if we don't want to admit it). And when other people don't comply, many of us hope that they feel terrible, too (and we usually don't like to admit that either). These feelings bring with them the urge to compare ourselves with others, which leads to the habit of benchmarking our worth against other people's abilities. Soon, pride develops, because we don't want to see that we can't be and do all that's expected of us. Rather than uncovering our limitations, we pretend that we've got it all together—when in reality, we're far from being on top of everything. Instead, we're trapped in a cycle of criticisms and judgments, stuck slinging "mud" (negative thoughts and comments) at those who don't share our values and opinions, and avoiding the muck that others throw our way.

Mudslinging not only separates us from those who aren't like us, it also hurts. It turns happy families (and thus, societies) into individuals too caught up in a cycle of retribution to focus on loving and accepting themselves and others. The result is that negative social trends arise, as they always do whenever there are consecutive generations in a given community who don't feel worthy or happy. When expectations and beliefs teach people to hate rather than love, conflicts arise and wars begin.

When an entire family has low self-worth, its members are highly critical, sarcastic, and judgmental of others, both inside and outside the group. Ironically, individuals trapped in the mudslinging cycle may be subconsciously aware of their inadequacies, but too caught up in their actions to recognize the effects.

Instead of stepping back and using kindness to solve their problems, they may overcompensate for their weaknesses by projecting an image of power and authority. Their fears are often locked in their deepest inner selves, as they refuse to recognize that anything within them is wrong or needs changing, and they've probably become proficient at playing the blame game. They not only fear seeing their deficiencies, they also fear change. Magnify this dread times the number of people in a family (or in a community of families), and that's how much energy you're likely to run into as you open the door on your family's closet of fears.

Consider Christopher Columbus and his battle to convince his community that India could be reached by sailing west, rather than east. Today we take this simple truth for granted. In the 15th century, however, most people believed that this was impossible. They thought that monsters waited for anybody who sailed outside the limits of known territory and laughed at those who dared to think that the world extended beyond their experience.

Although difficult at times, the end result of acknowledging and overcoming fears and gaining greater knowledge is growth, opportunity, and freedom. Without such progress, we're trapped. When we're too afraid to see, hear, or learn something new about ourselves, we're like the people of the 15th century who locked themselves within the confines of their limited knowledge because they were afraid—and their doubts were based on false information. Just imagine what could have happened if everyone was still stuck in that old geographical belief system!

The Dangers of Mudslinging

To encourage you, I'd like to share a few stories about the negative consequences of mudslinging and the positive results of overcoming it. In each case, much pain could have been avoided by closely examining what was being taught and the assumptions that were being made.

Sticking to the Rules: Jane and Miss Jones

My close friend Jane shared an experience she had in the sixth grade that caused her emotional pain way into her 30s. She had a teacher named Miss Jones, who was very particular about classroom rules and used them to publicly motivate (or humiliate) her students. This teacher read grades aloud and praised or condemned students in front of their peers; she also had a rule that all the children in her class must write their full names on their exams. If they didn't, she promised to fail them.

Jane liked to make good grades. She was a smart girl, and she felt good about herself when she excelled in school. She, too, felt safe and comfortable with rules, and she was raised in a family where obedience was important. But these two people butted heads when Miss

Jones's expectations crossed my friend's need and desire to excel in school.

Jane had a test coming up, and she studied hard, wanting to get a perfect score. She confidently took her exam and turned it in, believing it was flawless. Because she was so excited about her presumed success, she handed it to Miss Jones without writing her entire last name—she simply wrote her first name and last initial. Innocently, she broke the class rule.

The next day, when Jane was sitting in her seat expectantly waiting to hear her *A* announced to the entire class, she was shocked and horrified to hear her teacher announce that she'd failed. Miss Jones probably didn't realize it at the time, but she'd just flung a fistful of mud.

Jane told me, "I tried hard to fight back the tears so that no one would see me. I felt worthless and humiliated in front of my peers. I'd worked so hard to study for that test, and my reward was wiped away because my full name wasn't written at the top. I'd only missed two questions—I'd gotten an *A*. But because I didn't meet all of my teacher's expectations, I was humiliated and left to feel like a bad child in front of my entire class."

Jane's mother was angry when she found out what had happened and immediately marched to the school to complain. The principal got involved, but Miss Jones handled the problem by standing by her policy. She felt attacked, and responded by defending her position.

Regrettably, this attempt to help only caused more stress. Jane exclaimed, "How I wished that my mother had stayed out of it! The teacher was angry with me because her rules had been publicly questioned, and I had to live with her silent punishment—the pressure was almost too much to bear."

Although we don't know for sure what Miss Jones was thinking and feeling, we can assume a few possibilities. For one, we know that Miss Jones broke out in a stress-related rash during this crisis. It's possible that she was as upset about the whole thing as Jane was, and she may have struggled with her own feelings of worthiness. She probably had high expectations of herself, and likewise held her students to the same code. She may have grown up in an environment where rules were all that mattered.

There's nothing wrong with setting and maintaining high standards, but it's not healthy to attack another's personal worthiness when that individual doesn't comply. We're all human; none of us is perfect. It's likely that we'll never come close to measuring up if somewhere inside ourselves we feel worthless. Also, the problem for Jane wasn't the rule—it was the mudslinging. When others fail to meet our expectations, we're best served by deciding to understand and love one another rather than going on the offensive.

Sadly, Jane felt unworthy and overly responsible for years. This experience led her to make some important decisions about herself and her world that affected her life and family for a long time. First, she decided that her opinion didn't matter. Despite her efforts (and her Mom's) to explain her position to her teacher, she wasn't heard or validated. Second, she resolved that authority figures wouldn't listen to her, and consequently, she wasn't good enough to be heard. And third, she determined that it's better not to speak up and rock the boat, since doing so had only made things worse.

Because of these decisions, Jane lived her life fearing conflicts, trying to get everything right, and being terrified that she might not be valuable enough to be heard. If she hadn't changed, she would have taught this to her children, and over time, the responding behavior would have become a dysfunctional family pattern.

This story is unfortunate for both Jane and Miss Jones. The teacher's expectations weren't met, but rather than skip past the rule and see what really mattered, she chose to sling mud at her student. Jane, not knowing any better, accepted this. It's likely that both of them walked away from the situation feeling stressed, sad, and worthless. It was particularly damaging because my friend was only a child, making her vulnerable to her teacher's attitude and opinion.

Family Patterns: Spencer and Taylor

Another example of this harmful behavior comes from Spencer, a man I counseled who was born into a physically and verbally abusive home—his family was full of big-time mudslingers. He'd been heavily spanked and smacked and sometimes kicked, as well as verbally abused with excessive sarcasm and criticism. His family group feared imperfection and consequently criticized anyone who wasn't perfect (in their opinion), particularly themselves. It was commonplace to throw a verbal dart here and there, and they seldom praised others.

Nearly all of Spencer's family suffered from depression. My client's critical nature was ingrained and left him exceedingly sarcastic and judgmental. Consequently, he was unhappy, and his personal relationships suffered. He came to me hoping to change the way he'd been taught to interact.

During a counseling session, a visual popped into my mind that provided a helpful analogy: I saw people associating together in a greenhouse that was covered in a black tarp. No light was coming in, and all the plants were dead. Yet everyone inside was admiring the dead sticks, convincing each other that their greenhouse was the best—much better than all the others. Everyone was terrified to leave, because doing so meant they'd have to admit that everything was dead, and there was really no light inside.

I equated the sunshine needed to make the plants flourish with the love needed to make people and relationships grow; sometimes we convince ourselves that we're getting affection when we're not. This is common with families and communities where abuse is prevalent. We don't always want to see that our actions (or those of our leaders or family members) are unkind and potentially abusive. We want so badly to be cared for and connected to someone that, rather than facing the pain and fear, we adjust our perception of love to fit the dysfunctional patterns.

After many sessions, Spencer began to change his instinct to mudsling, as he realized that his family's pattern of sarcastically criticizing others didn't serve anyone. One day, his brother Taylor came for a visit; Taylor was very thin, and my client had put on a few pounds. The two went fishing and during casual conversation, Spencer's brother threw a dart by saying, "I guess you couldn't help it if the milk man was fat." Although the comment was spoken in fun, it hurt.

Everyone in their family was thin, and they regularly criticized overweight people. Spencer felt terrible about himself for gaining some weight and began to question his value. In defense, he spent the remainder of the visit trying to come up with comments that were equally sarcastic, rude, and critical. He knocked his brother at every turn, hoping to put him down so that he could feel better.

After Taylor left, Spencer came to see me. He was shifting back into a depressed state because he'd slipped into the family's unhealthy pattern. When good, healthy, and safe interpersonal communication can't exist inside a home, relationships fade and fail, eventually becoming only superficial in nature. Instead of talking about what's really going on inside of us, we discuss less risky topics, such as weather and sports. Even though Spencer loved his brother, the mudslinging had placed a gap in their relationship. In fact, the void was present in the whole family and prevented others in the group from feeling loved and accepted.

Life Choices: Two Couples at Work and Play

Carrie and Robert were close friends with Kate and Matt. Robert was a surgeon; his parents were hardworking, and his father was a physician, too. His family taught him that good people put in a lot of effort and contribute diligently to society. He assumed that people are bad when they focus on themselves and don't work hard.

Carrie, Robert's wife, had lived with Kate in college, and the two were best friends. Kate's parents were also hardworking, and her father was a doctor, too. She inherited a lot of money from her parents, whom she loved, but the truth was that she resented the time her father had spent away from home. Consequently, Kate had made a conscious decision to throw in the towel on this family pattern. She'd decided to spend more of her life living in the moment and having fun, so she was thrilled to meet Matt—a man who shared her desires.

Initially, when Robert met Kate and Matt, he didn't like them at all. For several years, every time the couples would interact, Robert would leave, slinging mud behind their backs as he went. He thought they were irresponsible, childlike, and ridiculous. Carrie would fruitlessly argue and defend her friends.

Finally, the two couples went on a weekend getaway together. Expecting to be frustrated, Robert was surprised when, over time, he began to enjoy Kate and Matt. Their fun-loving nature was a breath of fresh air for him, because he was tired and overworked. He had a hard time admitting it at first, but he finally said to Carrie, "I think Kate and Matt have it all figured out! I need to stop working so hard, learn how to play, and spend more time with my children."

Robert's family pattern had prevented him from accepting and enjoying his wife's friends for a long time, just as our judgments of others are often unfounded, standing between us and people we might otherwise come to enjoy and learn from. Kate and Matt became role models for Robert as he learned to balance work and play. Similarly, those who don't share our values can almost always offer us ideas for new ways of being. Just because a pattern, belief, or behavior is different, that doesn't mean it's bad. The world would be a dull place if we were all alike.

Facing the Fears That Hold Up the Wall

Earlier in the book, I told you about my husband, Shane, and the wall he'd created from his family's tradition that hard work was the only way to get what you want, and that trying something else could mean failure. I also mentioned that Shane liked the barrier; it made him feel better than those who didn't work as hard as he did.

Can you see the cycle? It goes like this: Maintain the code, sling mud at those who don't work as hard as you do, get nowhere, feel discouraged, recommit to working hard and following the family code, and so on. Behind every destructive family belief is a fear that distorts our perceptions and prompts us to make judgments. If you look closely at the stories about Jane, Spencer, and Robert, you can probably discover what it was that scared each of them.

Through my work, I've discovered that whatever the fear—failure, disappointment, rejection, abandonment, and the like—it's usually formed in the past. Many are inherited from our relatives and reside in the deepest parts of our subconscious. If they weren't resolved in our childhood, they continued to guide the creation of our perceptions as we grew. Consequently, these anxieties account for much of our unconscious patterning, which may dictate the majority of our choices, as well as the paths our children take as we pass these ideas along.

Distorted fears destroy family relationships over time, but ironically, many of us hang on to them because we falsely believe they help us achieve our goals. (Remember Shane's attachment to the wall?) In reality, if our beliefs originate from someone's worries, and they contradict growth and happiness, then they're faulty. We must cure them by unveiling their distortions; this is the only way to overcome sabotaging behavior.

So why do we participate in the interesting paradox of assuming that our behavior is helping us when it's actually the thing causing us the most harm? Because our natural way of dealing with our fears is to repress them—after all, they're scary. We'd rather hold on tight than face the bottom line. Consequently, and unknowingly, we come up with creative ways to hide the truth and pretend to still get what we want. That's why these patterns stick around for so long—we're unwilling to conquer the apprehension that creates them.

This was the case for a woman I worked with named Mary, who came to me after having been diagnosed with bipolar disorder. She was struggling financially, having trouble in her marriage, and didn't like being a mother.

Mary had been raised in a family that feared rejection, and she'd experienced some subtle abuse as a child. Like many kids in previous generations, she'd been hit and spanked when disobedient. In addition, she'd been occasionally blamed for the emotional state of the adults in her life (for example, "I wouldn't be angry all the time if you'd just be obedient."). As a result of this, she began discounting her self-worth early in life and decided that she was bad and unlovable.

Because Mary wasn't taught to face, uncover, or deal with her emotions, she held on to her family's fears for many years. She, too, feared rejection and blamed others' actions for her emotional upheavals.

Was she really terrible and unworthy of affection? No—in truth, she was a normal little girl who deserved love and learned by trial and error. Children aren't *bad* when they disobey; just as adults do, they learn by making mistakes. Mary felt that she needed more care and nurturing as a child, because the lack of it solidified her illusions about her value.

To her, the conclusions she made seemed logical—although I doubt that's what her parents wanted her to believe. I was acquainted with Mary's mom and dad, and they believed that they loved her very much. They felt that they were doing the best they could at the time with the parenting tools they had available to them. They wanted her to grow up to be happy and successful.

Mary, similar to my husband, had erected a brick wall based on false family traditions and inaccurate perceptions. When she finally reached the point where she wanted the barrier to crumble, she had to fight hard to convince herself to do it. She had, in fact, grown accustomed to the block.

Playing Victim

In a way, Mary was behaving like a victim when she really didn't need to. Similar to the young woman I mentioned earlier who cut off the ends of the ham because her mother and grandmother had, Mary was holding on to a belief that had been passed down to her.

It's true that she was a victim to some extent, but holding on to her fears of rejection had elevated that status. She'd begun to feel that she wasn't responsible for the outcome of her life. Since she deeply feared that she was unworthy and unlovable, she continued repressing her pain and believing that she was always the injured party. Ultimately, she created situations where she felt bad about herself and where she was treated poorly—in other words, her fears became her reality.

To Mary, it seemed easier to keep her wall rather than face all that she'd have to heal and change in order to get what she wanted most: happiness. She was more willing to live with her pain than confront it; she was a victim of her own beliefs.

As I worked with her, we talked about some important points. The questions I asked her can be helpful to anyone playing the victim of their own misperceptions:

- Can you really protect yourself from pain by allowing yourself to live in it rather than recognize it? Is that logical?

- Would you be happier if your anguish were to diminish or disappear altogether?

- Don't you believe that it's better to face your hurt and heal than live with it every day, carrying it into the future and risking passing it forward to generations that follow?

In our sessions, Mary answered these questions, and suddenly, she realized how ridiculous it was to hold on to her fear. Down came her wall! She realized that the fears and negative judgments didn't serve her. She let go when she uncovered the truth: The barricade was costing her happiness and success, not creating it. She discovered a new way to get what she wanted—one that really worked. She chose to heal from her pain, which naturally happened when she was honest with herself. Her suffering was released, and she healed a dysfunctional family pattern. And because of this, lots of lives improved.

Mary continued on this path for several years. With all parts of her consciousness working to support her, she went on to create financial security through various investments, and was a more effective leader and teacher. Most important, she became an outstanding wife and mother because she knew how to be honest, communicative, nurturing, and loving. Mary was brave, courageous, and smart! Healing our fears and judgments can appear scary and challenging, but it's always worth it.

Discovering Conflicts

Along with the brick walls we build due to false traditions and misperceptions, many of us tend to have conflicting thoughts and behaviors. Remember the Smith family? Some of the Smiths wanted to earn more, but the family belief system didn't support financial success. It subconsciously equated making a lot of money with prideful—or bad—behavior. The family members who wanted money also needed to feel loved and accepted by their relatives.

If we were members of the Smith family, it would be difficult to increase our incomes significantly because doing so might cost us what we want most: love and acceptance. But of course, income level really has nothing to do with whether or not we're worthy of affection.

When we're conflicted, we can rest assured that within our thought processes are fears that are costing us what we want the most. While working with me, my client Kim identified some of her fears about receiving financial abundance, since her goal was to make more money. She'd worked hard to let go of any beliefs that prevented her from increasing her income, but her situation wasn't changing.

At one session, I asked Kim to visualize climbing onto a crowded bus, where each passenger was to represent a different part of her. She described a variety of characters in the crowd, and then I asked, "Is there anyone there who doesn't support you in creating more wealth?"

Immediately, she said that inside her mind she saw three people stand up and contest her goal. I asked her to call on these parts of herself to explain their objections. She listened to each response and told me what she observed: She heard a part of herself declare, "It's bad to make money," and another stated, "You're not good enough to make more." The third aspect said, "I don't want any more money because making it means work, and I'm tired of working."

Right away, I could see how Kim was conflicted in these three ways about pursuing her goal. I kept asking questions about the visualization until we discovered more about her fears. First, the part of her that thought it was bad to have money said that she feared that others wouldn't accept her if she was wealthy. I suggested to Kim what I believe to be the truth: *It doesn't matter if others accept us, as long as we accept ourselves. As long as we do so, others will, too.* After all, this is the law of the harvest—what you put out comes back to you.

Then I asked the aspect of Kim that thought she wasn't good enough to experience abundance why she felt this way, and through contemplation, I came to understand that she felt unworthy. She didn't have as much money as she wanted, so she felt unsuccessful and less valuable than others. This was a complete paradox—a part of Kim was unwilling to receive what she thought would help her feel better about herself. Again, I suggested that it doesn't matter what others think of us, but only what we think of ourselves.

We addressed all the self-criticism that my client seemed to have, and as we did, she found that she was quite judgmental and frustrated. I tried to persuade her to accept herself and asked her to observe her many successes in order to free herself from all this condemnation. I suggested that if she loved herself and let go of her punishing thoughts, then perhaps she'd feel good enough and thus be more capable of creating what she wanted.

Last, I spoke to Kim about the part of herself that didn't want to work but preferred to have more fun. I suggested that she make a promise to bring more balance into her life by finding time each day to play. In turn, I encouraged her to support herself in making more money. I explained that if she allowed this to happen, she'd have more time to enjoy herself, go on vacation, and even pay others to help her when she needed assistance with her workload.

Being conflicted is common, and nearly everyone experiences it. When we don't have what we want, we can be certain that in some way we're unsure about what we want. As the saying goes, "If you always do what you always did, you'll always get what you always got." If we're finding it hard to fulfill our needs, there's something within us (most likely a thought process or belief governed by fear) that needs to change so that we can create a different reality.

After Kim's work with me, she understood that her self-esteem was directly attached to how hard she worked and how much money she made. She remembered that she was complimented as a child when she put in a lot of effort, although some of this pattern was her own decision, because she felt better about herself when she went the extra mile. Working hard is a good thing, but too little play is unhealthy; there's a need for balance in all things.

Associating her ability to do things with her self-worth wasn't a concept that Kim originated; both her parents supported this belief. Her mom and dad had struggled to create playtime, and when they did, they feared that they were doing something wrong—that they might be "bad" for relaxing.

Family belief systems always have a negative effect if they prompt us to attach our individual worth to a certain feature. We wind up picking on ourselves, and this translates into criticism of others. For example, if we judge ourselves as being unsuccessful for not making a lot of money, we may also view others as failures if they aren't wealthy. Our judgments lead us to criticize, which may affect the self-worth of someone we love, reinforcing a negative belief. Then we find ourselves caught in the mudslinging cycle that can be so damaging to our sense of well-being.

Learning Where to Look for Conflicts

Sometimes others mirror particular self-judgments for us. This typically happens when two people share the same negative belief. For instance, let's say that Dan is an associate at work and he shares the negative belief with Steve that *one must have money to be successful.* Dan doesn't make as much money as Steve, and because Dan holds this belief, he feels less successful and struggles to feel valued when he's around his co-worker.

Suppose that Steve makes a lot of money and has also attached his self-worth to his income. When he's around

Dan, the messages the two send to each other—both verbal and nonverbal—are critical. Dan resents Steve because he feels "less than," and Steve is harsh because he judges Dan and may fear being like him.

Consequently, their relationship will be uncomfortable. The two will push emotional buttons for each other on a regular basis. Dan might associate with others who make a lot of money and not feel bad about himself when they're around, but since Steve shares his beliefs, he mirrors Dan's judgments back to him. And Steve probably doesn't feel good about himself at these times either. Because they both hold this negative idea, they struggle to be loving, kind friends and associates to one another.

Most often, it's easier for us to spot the negative opinions of others than to see them in ourselves. That's why if someone "gets our goat" with their opinions, it's a good idea to look closely to see if they're reflecting back to us a similar judgment or negative assumption.

Very often, critical thoughts flow through our minds almost unconsciously. Perhaps we judge how our friends, neighbors, or loved ones raise their children, care for their yards, spend their money, communicate, clean their homes, take care of their families, and more. By paying attention to our assessments of others (and how our family members see them), we can begin to understand our own negative beliefs and fears and how they impact us.

Sometimes we judge others because we think doing so will help us feel better about ourselves. In fact, anytime we jump to conclusions about someone else, we become victim to the same judgment, and we may find ourselves living with self-debasement and filled with criticism. These thoughts reflect our fears, and the two support our negative convictions. If they remain unidentified, they'll cost us love and self-acceptance. Without these two key feelings, we can't progress toward caring for one another, and we won't have the ability to change our circumstances and get more of what we want.

The good news is that our judgments and fears, once uncovered, can help us understand the requirements we have for ourselves; they can help us discover our conflicted side. And when we heal our warring agendas, we can more effectively achieve our goals.

Conflicting Agendas in Marriage

Today's experts in marital relationships teach us that we unconsciously attract partners who carry behavioral and thought patterns that fit perfectly with our childhood wounds. In our efforts to heal the injured child within us, we tend to seek out individuals who demonstrate the behavior of our early caregivers. One of these experts, Dr. Harville Hendrix, Ph.D., expounds on this concept in his book *Getting the Love You Want.* He teaches that the other scenario is the process of marrying someone who reflects back to us a lost part of ourselves.

Knowing this, we can see that healing our marriages requires us to consider our family experiences and break free of any dysfunctional patterns that exist within them. I worked for a short time with a woman named Jean, who was very angry with her husband. She described him as forceful, powerful, angry, and controlling, while she described herself as easygoing, flexible, kind, and gentle.

Our conversation led us back to her childhood, where she uncovered an important decision she'd made. Jean lived in a family who believed it was bad to be angry, and so she'd decided that a good person avoids conflict. In an effort to gain the approval of her loved ones, she was obedient to the will of others and withheld her opinions. She was also afraid to express anger and share her thoughts. At an early age, she chose to shut down a very powerful part of herself.

After remembering her crucial decision, Jean began to understand how and why she ended up with an aggressive, forceful spouse. She'd buried a girl inside her who was just like he was, and his behavior was only a reflection of that child. It was time for Jean to see herself—even the hidden parts. We discussed her need to become more balanced by realizing that there are appropriate times to stand up for what you want and speak your mind, and that it isn't always necessary to keep the peace.

As difficult as he seemed, Jean's husband was actually a great teacher for her. When she began to appreciate his strengths and feel gratitude for the lessons she was learning from him, she subsequently began to notice a change in herself and her marriage.

As I mentioned earlier, blame is the process of shifting the focus from ourselves to someone else. When we project blame and don't take responsibility for our part in our relationships, we essentially forgo our power to create our lives in exactly the way we want them to be. We become victims to those who've hurt or offended us, and we don't have much power. It's my belief that most marriages can survive if each mate is willing to take a deep inward look. To really do this, however, the blame game must stop.

A common illusion that destroys couples is that our mates are responsible for our happiness. Since human nature leaves every person on the planet somewhat imperfect and unable to truly love unconditionally, it would be impossible for anyone to completely meet our needs, even if they wanted to try. Such high expectations are unrealistic and unattainable and lead to frustration.

When people start healing and changing family patterns, often they're tempted to leave a spouse or abandon a relationship. While sometimes that may be necessary, many times it isn't. One of the myths associated with divorce is the idea that leaving the marriage will result in more favorable circumstances. Many people who end things with their spouse have great hopes of eventually finding a perfect companion, but in reality, statistics show that second marriages have an even higher divorce rate than first marriages.[2] The odds of repeating the pattern of splitting up increase with every divorce.

Carl Gustav Jung, the distinguished psychologist, said, "Seldom, or perhaps never, does a marriage develop into an individual relationship smoothly and without crises; there is no coming to consciousness without pain."

Marriage is a union that brings together two individuals and splendidly allows us the experience (rocky or smooth) of becoming whole. As we work to heal couples that are deteriorating, understanding the family patterns that exist for both parties is key. Since it's almost impossible to change something we don't know about, it may be next to impossible to mend a marriage without a better understanding of the underlying conventions that may be causing the relationship to fall apart.

True joy comes from being whole, and a healthy alliance is the result of obtaining individual wellness first. When contemplating divorce, it's important that we look to ourselves to heal before we turn to our spouse. Coming to a clear understanding of our unconscious intentions and delicate personal needs will help us better know how to get exactly what we want. It's more difficult to create stability when we're unclear about what we want or if we're conflicted about relationships because of underlying fears we learned in our childhood homes. Many anxieties may reside inside our perceptions, and they might cost us a successful, intimate partnership if we're unwilling to take a closer look.

The Process

1. Noticing what your family does or doesn't value will give you more information about your limited beliefs and inherited patterns. As you become more aware of the connection between your judgments and values, you'll increase your ability to "listen between the lines" and hear the underlying messages that you send to other people and that your family sends to you.

    To begin the process, ask yourself these questions: *What do I judge in others? Do I judge the way they look, the way they dress, the type of home they live in, the kind of job they have, their level of education, their position in society, their religion, and so forth?* Make a written list of the private judgments you make toward the people with whom you associate—and be honest. Typically, we don't like to admit the critical thoughts that slip through our minds. But by being frank, you can experience breakthroughs in healing your family history.

2. Next on your list of judgments, record where your notion to think this way originated. Did your father, mother, grandparents, or other relative participate in similar beliefs? If so, write down where you learned the behavior.

    If you feel that these thoughts originated with you, ask yourself this question: *When, where, and why did I decide to hold these types of views?* Perhaps you decided as a child that fat people are bad and thin people are good, or perhaps you decided that having money was good or bad. Take as much time as you need to mentally explore those decisions, and then ask yourself: *Did I make this decision at a time when I felt insecure or unworthy?* If so, record what you feared the most about yourself when you made that decision.

3. Go back to the list of family beliefs that you began in the process at the end of the last chapter. Add any new ones that you've identified by answering the previous two questions.

4. Now, review your entire list of limited family beliefs and ask if each one originated because of a fear. Here's an example: Let's say that your mother felt rejected by her father, and she assumed he rejected her because she was overweight. Consequently, she became preoccupied with being thin and taught you that good people are thin and bad people are fat. As a result, you became judgmental about overweight people.

    In this example, your judgment would have been motivated by your mother's fear of rejection. Although she taught you to worry about being overweight, the real, underlying dread was of being unwanted. This belief might create the illusion that being thin makes a person acceptable. Uncovering the fears behind our judgments enables us to expose these types of illusions, so write down what you discover.

Chapter Three

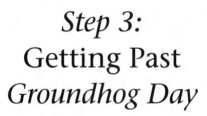

Step 3:
Getting Past
Groundhog Day

3

$\mathcal{T}$he movie *Groundhog Day* depicts the life of a man, played by actor Bill Murray, who wakes up to reexperience the same day over and over again. At first he's frustrated that he keeps having the exact same experiences at exactly the same times. Eventually, however, he perfects this day, learning lessons that enable him to move forward. At the conclusion of the movie, Bill Murray's character is more than grateful for the information he gained as he worked to move on.

Letting go of aspects of ourselves requires us to expand our awareness and understand something new. When we don't do so, we (and our families) live in our own versions of *Groundhog Day.* If the formula for change is so easy—*learn the lesson*—then why is it so difficult to transform our lives? Why aren't we running around begging for information, trying to discover more about ourselves, and willing to look deep within our consciousness so that we can create something new? Why do most of us live in our own version of an old television rerun and never seem to escape the same episode?

The primary reason may be that change is rarely comfortable. It means leaving our emotionally safe spaces, healing our fears, and releasing suffering (which is often our greatest worry). Searching our hearts or becoming conscious requires us to understand what scares us, to look into the past, and to feel our pain. Carl Jung once said, "The growth of the mind is the widening of the range of consciousness, and . . . each step forward has been a most painful and laborious achievement."

Kathryn Black, the author of *Mothering without a Map*, writes: "Examining our histories may well require a dive into dark waters, but by exploring those waters . . . we can leave them and the fear they evoke behind."[1]

Many times we know that we need to alter something, but we don't have any idea of *what* we need to do, and then we become afraid because we feel confused. As a result, we create resistance to change. When we don't change anything, however, we end up in a *Groundhog Day* scenario, as the cycle of fear and resistance repeats itself. To break this, we must have faith that pain is temporary and will pass.

The third step in the healing process, which is the subject of this chapter, will help you develop that faith. It may also be the part that takes the most effort, for it involves making four risky moves:

1. Moving out of your comfort zone and facing your fears

2. Working to discover any unmet needs and emotional insecurities holding you up, and then healing them by looking inward

3. Making a commitment to stop playing games and manipulating situations

4. Fighting the urge to always be in control by replacing that tendency with trust—in yourself

Moving Out of Your Comfort Zone

Nineteenth-century physiologist Claude Bernard once said, "Man can learn nothing unless he proceeds from the known to the unknown." In other words, growing requires movement beyond our comfort zones. A few years ago, a friend shared a story with me that illustrates this point. I have no idea if the events are factual or where the tale originated, but it has fantastic meaning:

> A man was held prisoner in a concentration camp during World War II. He violated one of the rules and was taken to an officer to receive punishment for his act. The officer pointed to a black door and said, "You have two choices. You can either go through the door on your left and face what's on the other side, or you can stand before the firing squad straight ahead."
>
> The prisoner opted to go before the firing squad. He was shot and killed.
>
> A guard who was standing by asked the officer, "What's behind the black door?"
>
> The officer responded, "Freedom." There was a moment of silence. Then he continued, "If someone has the courage to face the unknown, they deserve their freedom." He also noted that those who were given the choice had always picked the firing squad.

Why is it that the known feels so much safer than the unknown? For me, the black door represents facing what we fear most. For many of us, stepping out of our comfort zones often requires walking through such a portal. Since freedom is what we all naturally want, taking those uncertain steps is requisite to obtaining the kind of happiness we're searching for.

Learning Not to Resist

Often, life experiences begin to force us out of our family patterns (or comfort zone) and through the black door. When this happens, we have two choices: We can resist, or we can walk forward without looking back. I've learned that when circumstances press us to change, it's always more painful to balk.

A simple struggle with my son several years ago illustrated this truth. One afternoon he came to me with a small splinter in his hand, so I picked up the tweezers and began to explain that we needed to pull the splinter out. He was terrified. For about a half hour, I tried unsuccessfully to coax him into sitting still, and I finally held him down and extracted it.

His terror produced extraordinary amounts of opposition toward a small and insignificant experience. The matter could have been handled easily; however, because his fear created resistance, which led to pain and trauma, a seemingly insignificant moment became a drama. So it is with the family patterns that we hold on to and don't want to change. As we try to push away the inevitable because we're afraid of not being comfortable, we experience great anguish.

Perhaps the most important thing we need to realize is that our dysfunctional behaviors are usually part of our familiar comfort zones. Sometimes we're so used to unpleasant routines that we fight to keep them, simply because we know them so well. Similar to the man who faced the firing squad, we tend to choose pain because we know its parameters, and we fear that the unknown could be worse. So we get stuck in negative situations, and we resist altering them because what's uncomfortable is really comfortable—a total paradox!

Some people, in fact, don't feel at ease when they have what they want, because they're not familiar with the marvelous feeling of being abundantly blessed. If we truly long to fulfill our dreams, we must consider that we need to extend ourselves beyond our comfort zones.

Look to Your History for Comfort

Interestingly, a good place to start when you're about to push the limits of your comfort zone and embark on the healing process is with family-history work. You've learned that negative behaviors often stem from family traditions, so it's also true that positive behaviors have a similar origin. Studying your background to promote change can be painful, but it can also be healing. The simple work of exploring the past actually brings solace to many people, who then use that feeling to break out of dangerous, negative cycles.

Knowing your family's history will help you understand how you came to be and connect you with your family, which helps the group to heal collectively. For this reason, this exploration is a powerful and important way to bond the generations of the past to those of the present and the future.

Those who participate in such work find great satisfaction and joy as they discover names and stories of those who've come before. Some find a famous heritage, and many unveil stories of hardship. As we get to know more about our ancestors, our hearts are naturally drawn toward them, and we have a greater sense of belonging. Many claim to grow spiritually as they ponder the possibility of life after death and perhaps connecting with their loved ones on the other side. This link is the type of blessing that we often become willing to seek—even if we have to step outside our comfort zones and make a few changes before we can heal and start reflecting our family's positive history instead of the negative.

Discovering Unmet Needs and Emotional Insecurities and Healing Them Through Serving

One morning I had a phone call from a client who was struggling with her marriage. After a few minutes of discussion, we revisited a previous conclusion: She wasn't getting her needs met in the relationship. Later, I had several other conversations with her about the same subject, and as the day went on, a common denominator became apparent: All of us have unmet needs, and so do all families.

Our physical requirements are obvious: food, clothing, and shelter. We need to be cared for when we're sick and fed when we're infants, but we also have emotional and spiritual selves. Many people end up in therapy, live with depression, or exist in chaotic dysfunction—all some form of *Groundhog Day*—until they finally begin to recognize the powerful role of unmet emotional needs and work past them. Even those who grew up in ideal homes probably experienced occasions when they weren't nurtured perfectly.

As I help my clients discover their unmet needs, I typically suggest that they think of themselves as little children, then ask: *What did the child within me decide about myself and my world because my needs weren't met?*

My clients who've answered this question have always produced a list of beliefs that prove to be their core issues, which help us see many of their family's patterns of thought. Here are just a few of the answers I've heard:

- Sean, a man raised by a family with an abusive history, said, "I'm not a good boy. There's something wrong with me. I'm not able to get what I want. I hate myself." He was struggling to prove his worth in his career and to give and receive love in his relationships.

- Margaret, a woman raised by divorced parents, said, "I feel as if I'm going to die, as if there's no room for me to be heard or to be important. I feel unloved and powerless. I feel as if everything that goes wrong is my fault." She was suffering from depression.

- Joan, a religious woman raised in an ideal home, surprisingly answered, "I decided that I'm not good enough. I feel abandoned, all alone, and that I have to do everything myself. I feel like no one loves me because I'm not perfect." Joan was divorced and living alone. She'd been struggling with a pattern of perfectionism throughout her life.

- Tom, a man raised by a hardworking, middle-class family, said, "I decided that I had to work hard to get my needs met. I believed that the harder I worked, the better off I'd be. But then, one day, my father told me that it didn't matter how hard I worked, there'd never be enough money to meet my needs. As a result, I decided that no matter what I did, I'd never be successful." This comment was powerful information. Throughout his life, he'd experienced tremendous struggles on the path toward economic freedom and high achievement.

Tom was a man who'd worked extraordinarily hard to succeed in his career and, sadly, he seemed to fail over and over again. He could give me anecdote after anecdote of his hard work and how, despite all his amazing efforts, he was left without a dime, let alone any recognition or any success to claim as his own. This was a direct result of the beliefs he'd formed in childhood. Tom's father believed what he taught his son, and his grandfather believed the same thing. This was a dysfunctional family pattern of thinking.

Like Tom, Joan, Margaret, and Sean, discovering our unmet needs and then letting go of the resulting core beliefs allows us to get more of what we want. And in Tom's case, it was how he broke a negative family pattern.

Moving Past Emotional Insecurities

For others, negative family patterns can be broken only after emotional insecurities are faced. I worked with a tough, strong man named Oliver who didn't like coming to see me. For one, he didn't want anyone to know that he got help from a counselor. He was also terrified of his past, although he'd never admit it.

Unconsciously, he feared that a visit with me would take him back to the source of his problems, and he didn't want to go there. He wanted to prove that he could change on his own, without looking into his past. He was convinced that his belief system was fine and that there was nothing for him to uncover or resolve.

During his youth, Oliver had been abused and neglected by his mother. As is common with such children, he'd decided when he was only a boy that he must be bad—otherwise, his mom would have behaved more lovingly toward him. Not only did he feel rejected by his mother as a result of his abuse, but he'd also rejected the little boy still inside himself because of the assumption that he wasn't any good. He couldn't love himself.

Oliver subconsciously feared uncovering this childhood wound. As an adult, he projected a powerful, "better than" aura, but the child inside him felt small and bad. He didn't want anyone to see how terrible he was, so he protected his wound with denial and a harsh exterior.

Although he was a powerful man, he had unhealthy relationships. He was critical, intimidating, and cold—locked in a constant battle to force others to see how powerful and good he was. Oliver was controlling, and he had a hard time showing love to his wife and children. Inside, he felt out of control and, subsequently, he was depressed and didn't want to admit it.

In an effort to protect himself, Oliver buried his pain and consciously forgot much of his youth. Others didn't realize that he was hurting, and even he didn't recognize the depth of his own suffering until his life became so dysfunctional and chaotic that he was forced to acknowledge there was a problem. He lived in his own *Groundhog Day,* repeating his negative patterns until a crisis occurred:

His wife threatened divorce. This was his motivation to consider making changes.

At each of our sessions, Oliver would reluctantly delve into his past and examine old feelings, ideas, and beliefs. It took him a few years of sporadic appointments before he began a metamorphosis, but when he did, the transformation in him—and in his family—was profound. Through the process of healing the past, Oliver created a new life. He freed the little boy inside of him, finally giving himself the love and acceptance that he needed and deserved. As his self-care and happiness spread, he became a loving father, a compassionate husband, and a considerate and more effective leader at work.

Like Oliver, many of us are comfortable in our *Groundhog Day* scenarios until loved ones force us to look at things differently. The discomfort of our present lives is familiar and reliable, no matter how dysfunctional it may be. Often we, or the people we love, would rather not change.

In addition, many of us know that when we're healing our family histories and ourselves, things often get worse before they get better. This emotional upheaval can be difficult to face. It's comparable to cleaning out our closets and cabinets at home: We pull everything out and make a mess, and it can sometimes take days before we're able to put our rooms back together. Yet, when we're finished, we have greater order than before. Likewise, tearing things up is almost always part of the emotional cleanup process.

Here's another way to think about this difficult journey: Many years ago, just after the Easter holiday, we noticed an awful odor in my daughter's bedroom. After cleaning out every nook and cranny; washing bedding, clothes, and walls; and spraying nearly an entire can of Lysol everywhere, I resigned myself to the idea that there must be a dead mouse in the wall or the attic above her room. But before my husband began to tear down Sheetrock, I decided to go through her things just one more time. When I opened a side zipper pocket in an old suitcase hidden in the back of her closet, I found the culprit—rotten, dyed Easter eggs! This cute little girl had no idea that eggs spoil. She wanted to keep her precious treasures forever, so she'd tucked them safely in a secret hiding place.

If you've forgotten, I'll remind you: The odor from a rotten egg is nasty. There's no air freshener, incense, or potpourri capable of covering up its smell—and so it is with our dysfunctional and limiting beliefs. They may be innocently hidden in the emotional "suitcases" inside our subconscious. How did I know to look for something decaying in my daughter's room? The uncomfortable smell led me to it. How do we know to look for rotten thought processes and assumptions that stink up our lives? Our uncomfortable realities lead us to them.

When we don't clean out our emotional closets and aren't honest with ourselves about our emotions, our stinky issues may uncomfortably affect the lives of others. Our unwillingness to change may contribute to divorce, relationship failure, abuse, neglect, alcoholism, infidelity, and so forth. When we have core beliefs of unworthiness that are left unresolved, our natural tendency is to focus on ourselves. If we turn that attention to healing our hearts and cleaning up our messes, our honest look inward can be helpful and productive. As we mend our core feelings through love, we feel more affection toward ourselves—which cleans up our lives and gives us the ability to love and serve others.

The Power of Service

Albert Einstein once said, "Only a life lived for others is a life worthwhile." Once you've worked on yourself—healing your emotional ills and discovering your unmet needs—the quickest way to move forward and discover a happier you is by turning to others. Contentment is often commensurate with the service we freely render; many people claim the road to happiness comes through selfless acts of kindness and love. My husband (and many others) has found that when he's struggling with feelings of low self-worth, performing an act of service positively changes his mood, and his feelings of self-worth increase. More than that, he's discovered that many of the problems weighing heavily on his mind instantly resolve themselves when he provides loving aid to others.

When our lives are exceedingly dysfunctional, it becomes harder for us to give, but as we heal, we have greater opportunities to lift and assist those in need. Helping and lifting others often requires us to be on higher ground—to be stronger and more stable so that we can support our struggling neighbors, family, and friends.

By focusing our attention away from ourselves, we miraculously find that our needs are met. It's another paradox of this universe: We're filled as we look outward—we find ourselves fulfilled by giving, serving, and loving one another.

If we don't focus on healing our hearts and choose a selfish path, we may spend a lifetime pampering ourselves and never feeling worthy, appearing self-centered around our family and friends. We may not serve or love our spouse, focus on the needs of our kids or family members, or honestly care about friends and co-workers.

Depression is sure to set in as we draw inward and push others away.

When we truly care for ourselves, however, we have much to give. Our individual worth reveals itself as we generously donate our time, affection, and even money. The world needs love, and if we have some real sense of it within us, we can be of great service to our fellow man.

Recognizing That Manipulative Games Don't Work

In the process of healing, it's likely that you might run into a few obstacles—even after you've stepped outside your comfort zone and confronted your unmet needs. This is because we all play games when we don't know any other way to get what we want. Change is difficult, so sometimes we revert to easier methods of obtaining love or attention. Game playing—or manipulation— often starts when we're young as an innocent way to get noticed. For instance, a child may pretend to be sick in order to get attention from a parent.

Sadly, many adults do similar things for similar reasons, based on a subconscious notion that being unwell entitles one to love. I had a client who carried this belief throughout her childhood, and she consequently found herself facing a lifetime of illness trying to get love from her family.

It's possible that an early ancestor started this game. My client was descended from a woman who was a doctor, and it was believed that this great-great-grandmother gained her self-worth from caring for others. Unconsciously, she'd encouraged her family to be sick so that she could rescue them; this is how she validated her self-worth. My client was one of many family members who spent her life chronically ill. Her mother and siblings also played this game.

There *are,* indeed, payoffs for forming a manipulative game that uses disease to fill a variety of needs. To protect us, our subconscious minds can creatively organize something negative (being ill) into something that may feel positive (getting loved), even if it's costly. Bernie Siegel, M.D., points out in his best-selling book *Love, Medicine & Miracles*[2] that sickness can sometimes be an excuse for us to reject unwelcome assignments, duties, or jobs. It may give us permission to ignore our responsibilities or rest when we otherwise wouldn't allow ourselves to do so, and can serve as an excuse for failing.

Sometimes it creates time to do something we've always wanted to try. For example, being under the weather can allow us to take time off to reflect, meditate, and chart a new course. When we're sick, sometimes it's easier to request and accept love, express ourselves, or be honest about something.

But maybe, when we become more conscious of our game, we won't need disease to give us permission to get what we want or need. Rather, we can rearrange our priorities and change. We can make a conscious choice to spend a few days focusing on ourselves without using illness as an excuse.

While I was giving a seminar about manipulation in relationships, I met Sherrill. She raised her hand and complained about her ex-husband's need to control her through finances. She described him as manipulative and stingy and insisted he was playing games with his money. On the other hand, she characterized herself as kind and giving, claiming that she enjoyed sharing and wasn't worried about receiving anything in return. She insisted that she didn't control anyone financially and told me that her ex-husband had a lot of money, but she had very little. It was evident through her tone of voice that she judged him, especially with regard to this issue.

I responded to Sherrill's comments, suggesting that she might want to consider how his behavior was reflecting something back to her. I asked her specifically to look at her core beliefs (particularly her family patterns) about money. I explained that it was possible that her ex-husband held the same core beliefs; however, their responses might be different.

As is typical for most of us, she found it easier to peg her ex-husband's games than to notice her own. She said that he had deep self-worth issues, and that to compensate for them, he worked hard to make and hoard money. Having wealth helped him feel powerful and important. Sadly, no matter how hard he tried, his accumulation of capital never filled his emotional need for love and approval. His game left him in a destructive, self-perpetuating cycle of appearing selfish and feeling unworthy. Apparently, his behavior was a pattern that he'd learned from his family.

Then our focus turned to Sherrill. Close examination led us to understand that her unmet needs and fears were exactly the same as her ex-husband's: She also felt unworthy, underpowered, and unimportant. Her response, on the other hand, was to give her wealth away so that others would approve of her and find her important. But no matter how much she donated, she never filled the void within herself. Her selfish motive to be generous didn't make her feel better—in fact, it made her feel less worthy than others and unimportant. Our conversation helped her see how she projected an image of financial helplessness, appearing to be a victim in need of rescue.

If and when Sherrill tried to serve, her attempts weren't honest. She was never giving without any expectation of receiving. (That's a key element of service: To give freely, we must do it without requiring something. Otherwise our attempts wind up feeling manipulative.) Sherrill's ex-husband felt controlled by her continual need for cash, which was actually a plea for love, and he hated being financially manipulated by her.

We've all had the experience of going back to a place from our childhood: a playground, an elementary school, or even just the images in a photo album. It's amazing how different our view is when we're grown up and looking back. What once seemed scary, tall, and wide may actually be friendly, short, and skinny. I remember going back to Stenwood Elementary School in Vienna, Virginia, after many years of living far away. I imagined the halls would be wide and long, but I found narrow corridors in a building so small that the county had been forced to add trailers in the back to meet increased enrollment. Similarly, I've had clients tell me about slippery slides at local parks that seemed so tall in their memories, but when they returned as adults, the slides were amazingly short.

The games we play as families and as individuals that seem to meet our needs usually originate in youth, and they seem valid until logically examined. Under scrutiny, though, it almost always becomes clear that many childhood perceptions are limiting.

When we begin manipulating to fulfill our needs, we make it difficult to change because a part of us believes that the game works, and so we hold on. It's not until we uncover the flaws and understand the reasons why we're doing these things that we're really able to release them. And until we let go, we make it hard to fully transform our lives.

Relinquishing Control, Developing Trust

For many of us who are trying to heal, a final obstacle preventing us from getting past *Groundhog Day* is the need to control other people and situations. We usually do this because we're afraid of what will happen if we're not on top of everything. Of course, most people don't like to be ordered around, so conflict naturally arises as individuals scramble to gain command, and others fight to avoid them. Ultimately, those who attempt to rule others feel out of control themselves and usually wind up unhappy.

While on a weekend getaway with my husband, I observed a man at the airline ticket counter. He was stressed out and irritated because his plane was going to arrive late. I assumed that his anger was a secondary reaction to his fear, which is almost always the case. I could see that he probably felt afraid that he'd be late for his final destination. To compensate, he began to attempt to direct the situation and became agitated when he realized that he couldn't affect the timing of his flight. His emotional frenzy left him experiencing anxiety, and his frustration spread as his anger began upsetting those around him. He felt out of control, and so did many others who were trying to help him.

I noticed that he eventually made his flight, and I assumed that he later arrived at his destination, since

I didn't hear of any airplane crashes that day. I guessed that much of his stress was needless, because it was his attempt to control his external world that really left him feeling upset. And I believe that his fears weren't as important as the emotional energy he lost trying to force his way. Even if he'd missed a connecting flight, as many of us do, it's unlikely that the end result would have been as dramatic as his reactions in the airport.

As I said earlier, whenever we feel fear, we immediately have a need to master our environment, relationships, children, or even ourselves. We lose a lot of energy in the process, and perhaps more important, we move further and further away from experiencing the joy and connection that comes when we're able to love and trust others.

While we want to feel empowered over the course of our lives and thus be effective managers of ourselves, controlling never works—and fears are usually false. We aren't trusting people and situations when we're attempting to dictate them. My husband's brick wall, for instance, was the method that he used to protect himself from the pain of defeat. But as long as he kept it, he was powerless to create what he wanted, and he felt like a failure because of it.

Trust and faith are antidotes to control issues because they help us release the roadblocks set in our paths. Instead of worrying that our loved ones will fail, we can believe that they'll succeed, even when it looks as though they might not. Instead of fretting that situations won't go our way, we can have confidence that matters will work out well for us. By putting our energy into trust and faith rather than fear, we can be happy, feel empowered, and really support ourselves and others. We can avoid stress by expecting that all will come together in the end—and the truth is that it will.

I once worked with a woman named Elizabeth and her son, Don, who was struggling to make friends in elementary school. He frequently sat alone on the playground at recess. The family was obsessive about rules and schedules, and shared a belief that "heavily controlled environments produce freedom." Even though he was a child, Don relied on a rigid routine to feel safe. Because his comfort zone was confined to predictable situations, he wasn't confident with unstructured socializing.

His was learned; his mother functioned similarly. Although her social life was not as affected by her family beliefs, her need to be safe in a controlled environment kept her from being able to enjoy many activities that were spontaneous and fun. In fact, Elizabeth rarely took part in playful activities, instead confining herself to a rigid routine of hard work. She also felt depressed, was lacking self-love, and was stuck inside a confined comfort zone.

My client's instinct to control her family stemmed from intense, terrifying experiences from her youth. Her father left the family when she was young, abandoning her mother to raise six children on her own. Elizabeth spent a lot of time home alone. As the youngest child, she was often left to fend for herself while her mother was working and her siblings were out and about. Not only was she left physically, she felt alone emotionally, since her mother was distant after her father walked out on the family.

Elizabeth wanted to be loved and nurtured, but as it was, she felt deserted and neglected. Vowing not to abandon her own family, she went overboard with rules and structure. She wished that her childhood home had been safe and structured, but since it wasn't, she wanted to create that in her adult life—not only for her children, but for herself. Unconsciously, her children reminded her of the little girl inside her that was afraid to be alone. Consequently, she was terrified to let her kids grow up and move on.

Although Don hadn't personally suffered trauma, as long as his mom's fears remained, he continued feeling unsafe, insecure, and stuck. Elizabeth's feelings, and Don's adoption of them, left them both struggling to grow, needing to control in order to feel safe, and feeling conflicted about change, control, and freedom. As Elizabeth let go of the anxieties from her childhood, her son was able to release many fears and gain more self-confidence. The two worked together to heal these family patterns, and in doing so, they began enjoying happier lives. Particularly, Don's relationships at school improved, and he found himself befriended by other children on the playground at recess.

Although safety *can* be found within a controlled environment, when tremendous fear traps us into needing to rule others, the situation, or ourselves, we're blocked from moving forward, and we ultimately fail to experience a true sense of freedom or joy.

The Process

1. Earlier you answered the question: *What is it that I want the most in my life right now?* Take a minute to confirm that what you think you want is really what you desire. For instance, if you wrote down that you long for more money, ask yourself: *Why? What do I think I'll get if I have it?*

2. During a seminar, a client told me that what he wanted most was to buy a ranch. I asked him what he thought it would give him, and he said, "Freedom." A woman in the front row smiled, raised her hand, and quickly explained that having a ranch won't make anyone free. She grew up on such a property and knew that it was extremely demanding and a huge responsibility that really ties you down. My client wanted independence—not a ranch. The ranch only symbolized his idea of this ideal. If he found a sense of liberation inside, he'd probably enjoy having his own spread. However, if he never found that within himself, his external situation wouldn't matter, because he wouldn't have what he actually wanted.

    Explore your wants now, and search deep. Determine what it is that you *really* want the most.

3. Now ask yourself: *How do I go about getting what I dream of?* If you determine that you want more love (or a sense of self-love), look at the ways

you try to get it. Do you use addictive behaviors to help you feel better? Some people eat food or engage in sex to feel cared for, while many constantly seek the approval of others. They worry about the way they look, the clothes they wear, the job they have, or their social affiliations. Do you rely on the approval of others because you don't have enough self-love? Write down your answers.

4. Next, ask yourself: *Is my method of fulfilling my needs effective? Does it work?* Explore the ways your behaviors do and don't succeed. Ultimately, you must consider whether your methods of getting what you want are helping you toward your goal.

5. Although you may not like your present circumstances (living without whatever you most desire), identify all the reasons why your "uncomfortable" situation is actually somewhat "comfortable." For example, I may want to earn more money without working so hard for it, but I may be comfortable putting in the hours and struggling financially because I feel good about myself when I have to labor to get what I want. Or, I may want more self-love, but I'm comfortable with my addictive behaviors because they mask my pain, and so I don't want to change. Make a list of *your* false comforts.

6. Take a look into your past. Please review your answer to the question I posed earlier in this

chapter: *What did I decide about life and my-self when my needs weren't met as a child?* Your responses will help you identify your core beliefs. When I looked at this question myself, I realized that I'd developed the core belief that I was bad and others were good. I assumed that everyone else in my world seemed to be getting his or her needs met, but since I wasn't, something must be wrong with me. Consider how your core beliefs correlate with your family patterns. Is it possible that your parents or grandparents shared your ideas? If so, are any of these assumptions limiting family patterns? Make notes during this exercise.

7. Finally, take a moment to meditate. Visualize pulling out all the energy that stands between you and what you want the most, forming it into a shape, and giving it a color. Look closely at the image inside your mind. Ask yourself: *Why do I want to keep this shape?* Make a mental note of your answers, and then ask: *How does this obstacle help me fulfill my needs?* Use your replies to help determine how the object falsely appears to get you what you want. Examine how the form actually prevents you from moving forward.

   When you're ready to let go, once again visualize the shape. Watch inside your mind as the image is cast into the light of the sun, where it explodes and transforms into positive energy. If any part of you wants to hang on, or if you see the object come back again, keep asking yourself how it falsely seems helpful. When you uncover all the illusions, you'll naturally want to release them. This will help you turn the page on *Groundhog Day* and move to the days that follow.

Chapter Four

Step 4:
Finding the Treasure

4

$\mathscr{T}$he world's largest gold Buddha statue—which is more than 700 years old, weighs approximately 5.5 tons, and is worth about $14 million in United States currency—was once hidden away, its true value remaining undiscovered for a very long time. The object has a colorful history: The Golden Buddha, as it's known, was cast in Thailand in the 13th century. At some point, it was covered in plaster (most likely in an attempt to hide the valuable icon from thieves or looters), but the disguise was so good that everyone apparently forgot what was hidden beneath. King Rama III had the plaster-covered statue moved to Bangkok and installed in a temple; over time, the site was neglected and then completely abandoned around 1931.

The true nature of this sculpture wasn't discovered until it was moved to its present location at Wat Traimit in 1955. When it was being prepared for the transfer, some of the plaster chipped off, revealing the gold underneath. The workers were astounded by what they'd uncovered.

Like the Golden Buddha, our true natures are often covered, and even entirely forgotten. Sometimes they're hidden for good reasons—for example, we may create phony exteriors to protect ourselves. But in the end, these façades only keep others (and us) from recognizing our real value.

Life has a way of chipping through the plaster, however. Although hard times may seem to damage us, challenging experiences can begin a process of revealing our golden interiors. And isn't it best for everyone when our true worth shines forth? Being honest about who we really are allows us to harvest our treasures.

Step 4 in the healing process will help you figure out who you are underneath. You can chip away at that plaster by finding value in opposition, turning weaknesses into strengths, overcoming codependent behavior, learning how to forgive, and being willing to change your opinions if needed.

Opposition Leads to Growth

An anonymous writer once said, "People don't grow old. When they stop growing, they become old." The universe is made up of matter that eventually breaks down. Different elements combine to form opposition, and despite our efforts to heal and recover, there is lack in the process. We age because we can't keep up with the rate at which we need to repair or heal.

Have you ever known an older person who seems young—who still thirsts for knowledge, loves to learn and play, and embraces growth and change? Despite their wrinkles, does this person seem old to you? Age is relative: Young people can seem worn-out if their spirits die, and their desire for progression and greater knowledge is gone.

What does all this mean for you and me? Well, I believe that we need to use opposition in our favor, taking the bad things that happen to us and using them to grow. After all, without darkness, how can we recognize—or appreciate—light? Without sadness, how can we truly know what it means to have joy? Without fear, how can we understand trust? Just as our bodies are forced to react to the natural results of aging, our souls must face the opposing forces that sometimes bring us down. Similar to those who age gracefully, we can learn to react to opposition gracefully, using it to help us recognize our blessings and grow from our experiences.

Dr. Deepak Chopra, the author of the international best-selling book *Ageless Body, Timeless Mind,* writes: "If there is anything natural and inevitable about the aging process, it cannot be known until the chains of our old beliefs are broken."[1]

Learning from Negative Patterns

Negative family patterns—even destructive ones—hold treasures for us. Every minus can be seen as a plus as we advance through life, although sometimes we struggle to believe this. It's common and natural for us to be afraid to see the good in our trials, because we don't want to approve of the very things that have caused us pain. Learning to interpret troubles in a positive way can be a difficult process. But by uncovering the illusions and finding the gifts they've masked, we can grow, and begin to feel more love and gratitude for our relatives. This is the true healing process.

Family members rarely intend to do each other harm. In fact, their actions typically are founded on love. For instance, one of my clients was descended from a man who didn't feel adequate because he had no formal education. Consequently, he pushed his children and grandchildren to become "good" by attending Ivy League colleges. Although he wanted the best for them, he instilled self-doubt in his descendants. Once my client understood the love behind her grandfather's push for excellence, her anxiety about failing—which had plagued her throughout her life—dissipated.

The primary treasure of this legacy was the opportunity to excel academically. When the pattern was identified and healed, however, she was able to realize that her grandfather had also given her an opportunity to understand the pain of self-doubt and gain a greater knowledge of her individual worth.

Learning from Weaknesses

Just as you can learn from opposition and its accompanying negative experiences, you can also gain wisdom from those traits you *believe* to be your weaknesses. This is important because they help make you who you are—so you might as well turn them into strengths or at least gain something from them. Judging a shortcoming as bad ultimately means that you're rejecting a part of yourself. For instance, if I'm impatient and demand a lot of myself and others, and I don't like this quality, I may decide that these characteristics are always terrible. Under the appropriate circumstances, however, they could be my strength. For a corporate leader, an impatient and demanding personality might make the difference in whether or not the company succeeds. Of course, it's possible that a spouse may not appreciate these qualities as much as the stockholders, but that's why we have the ability to redirect these traits and use them in the situations best suited to showing their strong points.

A magical thing happens when we stop expending large amounts of energy ignoring and hiding the parts of ourselves that we don't like: We begin finding the gifts in our weaknesses, and we learn to be more giving. Because it's necessary that we care for ourselves before we can reach out to others, the process of accepting all aspects of our personalities supports our efforts to love unconditionally, beginning with ourselves.

Let the Beach Ball Float Up and Away

In *The Dark Side of the Light Chasers,* author Debbie Ford discusses the process of embracing our weaknesses, which she calls the shadow side of our personalities.[2] She describes how the things we detest about ourselves can undermine our feelings of worthiness, and how it's natural, when face-to-face with our dark side, to turn away or make an arrangement with it to leave us alone. She points out, however, that when we do this, we unintentionally lock away some of our most valuable resources. These attributes try to surface and get our attention—we can use them to better ourselves—but because we're afraid to face them, we expend a lot of energy keeping them locked up.

In the process, we end up feeling more and more unworthy. Like a giant beach ball that we can no longer hold under water, these aspects pop back to the surface whenever the pressure is removed. When we stop working at hiding parts of ourselves, like the beach ball, they have the opportunity to float up and drift away.

Families often hide their troublesome issues because of pride and fear, but doing so leads to dishonesty. And emotional untruth prevents us from growing and healing. Eventually, everything will surface, even if it takes years. It may feel scary to the family to be honest, but doing so is necessary in order to create emotionally healthy and happy homes. Similar to the beach ball, it all needs to float to the surface for the family to heal.

When a general is planning a battle, he studies the weaknesses of his army as much as he bolsters its strengths. If he ignores his shortcomings and only focuses on his strong points, he's apt to lose—and vice versa. This isn't just military strategy. A good athlete or coach will perfect a game by studying both the highs and lows of the opponent and themselves.

Knowing both our negative and positive traits empowers us to be successful at the game of life. Do we know our weaknesses, or do we hide them in a closet and pretend (hope) they don't exist? Do we know our strengths, or do we keep them secret, fearing rejection (from ourselves or others) if we truly own our God-given gifts and talents?

Our ability to truly succeed depends on our willingness to understand, own, and accept ourselves—both the good and the bad. As we come to terms with ourselves, we also learn to embrace our families.

Letting Go by Giving Back:
Healing from Patterns of Abuse and Codependency

Changing weaknesses into strengths will go a long way toward healing negative behaviors. There are some family patterns, however, that need specialized, individual work to heal. These are the ones that exist because of abuse and codependency.

Mental, physical, or sexual abuse can cause severe, permanent consequences for victims and their families. Those who were mistreated experience fear, depression, guilt, self-hatred, and low self-esteem, and they often alienate themselves from healthy relationships. When aggravated by continued abuse, powerful emotions of rebellion, anger, and hatred can come to life. These feelings are typically directed inward, and they impact the way that victims see others, life, and even God.

Frustrated efforts to fight back can collapse into drug abuse, addictive behaviors, abandonment, and in extreme cases, suicide. Unless healed, this leads to despondent lives and inharmonious marriages—and these patterns typically get passed down a family line. If healed, though, the beauty that dwells within each person can be revealed, breaking away the plaster that has covered it for years.

To begin recovering, victims must first come to know that abuse happens because of *another's* wrongful attack on their personal freedoms; victims aren't responsible for what happened. And most important, freedom can be regained. We all have the power to choose to forgive, and in doing so, we give back the painful wound to the one who is ultimately responsible—the abuser. We're then free to move on because we've removed a burden.

This is exceedingly difficult to do. Deep down, most of us probably fear that if we forgive, we approve of the action. But I prefer to think of it as something you actually *give*: You *give* the burden back to the abuser. You refuse to turn to hate and anger—which were probably involved in the perpetrator's actions. You return your rage and move on. After all, much of what happens in such a situation is that the abuser transfers his painful state to the victim. If you give this back, you have the opportunity to break free.

When Abuse Leads to Codependency

When abuse isn't forgiven or healed, the natural result is codependency. Many times, the harmful behavior occurred a generation or more in the past, but the unhealthy bonds it inspired lives on. This is common, even though it's destructive and disables marriages and children. Psychologist James J. Jones describes this type of relationship in his book *Let's Fix the Kids:*

> Codependency is perhaps best understood as a dysfunctional pattern of living characterized by confusion about one's identity and an over-attentiveness to the problems, needs, feelings, and opinions of others. . . . Codependency means that we are focused on somebody else's issues and problems, and their life becomes the most important factor in our own life. We see ourselves as unimportant; feel guilty and selfish for focusing on our own feelings, needs or wants, and lose contact with what we think or believe. A codependent is someone who feels responsible for others, someone who wants to fix, rescue, and make everything okay in the family. . . . Codependent persons are more concerned about what other people think and feel than they are about what they themselves think and feel. A codependent has lost sight of his own person, his own self. In homes where the parents are dysfunctional, critical, perfectionists or have unrealistic expectations

for their children, the children can become confused about boundaries. The children try to gain acceptance by doing what the parent wants, and thereby lose sight of what they want. Boundary confusion is one of the foundation blocks upon which a dysfunctional, codependent personality is developed.[3]

The story of struggle and strength depicted in the process of a baby bird breaking open its eggshell is a metaphor that reflects a message directly to you and me, but particularly to those of us who are codependent. We need to face our struggles independently in order to be strong and survive in our world. We must break free on our own, without expecting others to be responsible for our lives or our behavior. Merging our energy with other people by attempting to rescue them or gain their approval prevents the strength that comes from the effort and eventually disables us. Staking your independence and claiming responsibility, however, breeds success.

If you're living in a codependent relationship, the first step to healing is to take responsibility for choosing to participate in perpetuating a destructive family pattern. Figure out what you're doing to keep the cycle going, and then examine how others might be contributing, and forgive them. Set yourself free from worrying about their decisions and motivations. Instead, focus on keeping your motives pure and your decisions based on love.

Some individuals fear that they'll be in trouble if they give back what's been wrongfully dumped on them, but this isn't true. We don't help others by taking responsibility for their problems. Rather, we deny our loved ones opportunities to grow and learn when we don't allow them to be accountable for their faults or weaknesses. The fact is that you'll feel much better toward your parents and your more-distant ancestors if you aren't carrying around the weight of their burdens. You can have greater compassion for them when you let them be responsible for what they created, and go forward living a happy, fruitful, and productive life.

You'll be amazed by the freedom that comes when you allow yourself to release the burdens caused by other people's abuses and addictions. Because these aren't your fault, it's not necessary to carry them forever. Forgive and take responsibility by choosing to learn and grow from your trials and deciding to move forward in spite of them.

Make Your Home a Safe Haven

Norman Bodek, coauthor of *The Idea Generator*[4] and president of PCS Press, wrote a short article that interested me. In it, he said, "Watch a baby when she/he first learns to stand. The idea comes, the baby struggles, reaches, holds on, and miraculously stands—then crashes down. The process is repeated over and over again. Eventually, the brain learns the perfect way to stand, remembers it, implants it. Then, standing is done without thought, or struggle."[5] The baby moves on to walking and getting into all the trouble a little one can make. Bodek confirms what most of us know about the process of learning: It comes from making mistakes. So if we can't commit or admit errors, we prevent ourselves from learning and growing.

Another important step to healing and thus uncovering the treasure within yourself, your children, and other family members is to make your home a safe haven. Fill it with love—and let those you cherish know that mistakes are inevitable and acceptable. Whenever we mess up, our failings offer others a chance to learn as well. When we realize that we get affection when we have self-acceptance, our ability to learn and grow is significantly enhanced, as is our ability to create caring homes and families. And as we get to this point, we begin to see even more clearly the gold that lies within us.

Life produces a variety of dramatic stories that leave us wanting one thing: more love. Most folks are doing the very best they can, and all they desire is to be cared for—especially at home. But many people don't realize what they're seeking, so they falsely perceive that more wealth, control of others, or the transient pleasures of addictive behaviors will make them feel happy and fulfilled. And often, money, fame, and career success—or the use of drugs, alcohol, cigarettes, or prescription medications—do bring the *illusion* of acceptance, freedom, and affection. Only when these individuals peel away the motivations that leave them participating in destructive behaviors do they identify their real needs. Almost always, deep down, what they want is to be loved by their families more than they want and need to be adored by anyone else.

Often I ask my clients this question: *What is it that you want the most?* If they answer with a physical item, such as a new car, a house, or more money, I ask them one more question: *If you have that object, what does it get you?* More often than not, when people uncover their reasoning, they find that they want love and acceptance more than anything.

When there's a lack of tenderness, people feel unworthy, and this kind of pain prompts destruction. Those who commit grievous crimes are often brokenhearted individuals who are desperately seeking real affection from the world around them, secretly hating themselves, and not aware of a way out of their anguish.

Joe, a man I became familiar with through my church, had a childhood that was filled with rejection, abuse, and emotional trauma. His deep lack of self-love (a family pattern) caused him to attract negative situations and unhappy, angry people. Over time, he became a drug dealer and was heavily addicted to cocaine—it was a miserable life. He desperately prayed to God one night, begging for a miracle to occur so that he could get out of the hell he'd created. Within two days, the police broke down his door and arrested him.

He'd never expected this to be the answer to his prayer! Yet the prison sentence that followed gave his body time to clean up the toxicity in his system and allowed him to gain a sense of life outside the distorted world of drugs. Prison turned out to be a blessing.

This man had a life of crime, but what did he want the most? Love and acceptance. Although he'd found ways to cover the hurt that seemed to be connections to peace and affection, they ultimately resulted in more suffering and a cycle of destruction. Only by honestly confronting his pain did he begin to chip away at the plaster hiding the golden treasure of his soul.

A similar story of a criminal transforming is told in the life and character of Jean Valjean in Victor Hugo's book *Les Misérables*. This hard-hearted man, jailed for 19 years for stealing a loaf of bread, is ostracized by society when he's released from prison. Subsequently, he's marked for failure. A loving priest embraces the opportunity to guide and care for him, and Valjean is forever changed. He gains a new identity, becomes financially successful, contributes to society, and develops a strong and healing relationship with a child, Cosette, whom he raises as his daughter. The story is touching and demonstrates that even those who appear unfeeling may be kind when understood, embraced, and given an opportunity to serve.

Essential Values for Successful Families

Successful marriages and families are established and maintained when those involved incorporate values such as forgiveness, respect, love, and compassion. Earlier in the chapter, I discussed the need to forgive in the context of abusive situations and codependency, which require a lot of work to heal. But even the little things need absolution if we really want to break the cycle and start a new tomorrow. In order to heal our dysfunctional patterns, we must learn to forgive everyone who may have wronged us: those who've taught us ineffective ways to think, behave, and believe, and the people we blame for causing us sorrow or making us doubt.

Why? Because when we can't stop blaming, we naturally hold on, which causes more pain. It enables our wounds to fester, rot, and promote separation from those we love. But forgiveness is a powerful tool—in fact, it's a blessing. There's nothing more rejuvenating than a heart that pardons and is ready to overcome the mistakes of the past, be they small or profoundly serious.

As you implement this in your family, the natural results will be a home full of more respect, kindness, and compassion, and these are certainly values worth passing on to those you love. After years of research, a study showed that the single most important ingredient in a happy home is kindness.[6] The study says that it's not thoughtful tasks that do the trick, it's kind people—and there's a difference.

Those who are charitable by nature and concerned with the long-term welfare of others in thought, word, and deed, will contribute to the continued happiness of the family. To some, it may seem old-fashioned to speak of these values—forgiveness, respect, love, and compassion—but these are the qualities that have built great families. Even today, they point the way by which we may find happiness. They act as anchors in our lives, in spite of the trials, tragedies, and cruelties that can leave us suffering. The truth is that we can't be content without them.

J. C. Friedrich von Schiller said, "Every man stamps his value on himself. The price we challenge for ourselves is given us by others—man is made great or little by his own will." A client once said to me, "I feel that I'm able to love my husband, children, ancestors, friends, and neighbors. Why? Because I've gained self-respect by healing my dysfunctional patterns—so much so that I can say that I've truly learned to love myself."

When we heal, we love, which makes us forgiving, respectful, considerate, and compassionate. Mending our lives allows these values to expand, and then they help us foster and maintain happy and successful families.

Seeing Others as God Sees Them

The opinions we hold about others—such as "My husband is lazy," "My daughter is irresponsible," "My father doesn't listen," or "My brother is cynical"—suggest to these individuals that they embody these patterns of behavior. You can actually contribute to another's actions by supporting them in maintaining limited perceptions of themselves. If you stop supporting these negative qualities and send positive messages instead, those you love may cease needing confirmation that they're "worthless," "irresponsible," or whatever unpleasant characteristic you once projected upon them. Something as simple as holding back a judgmental opinion has the ability to allow others to change and blossom; it also helps us better ourselves, thus getting closer to the treasure within.

The power we have to direct other people's behavior through our unconscious beliefs was made clear to me when a woman named Lindsey called to make an appointment and an interesting thing happened. She mentioned her name several times in our conversation, but for some reason, I just couldn't remember it! I was embarrassed when I hung up the phone and realized that I hadn't written down her first name. I didn't want to call her back to ask, because I didn't want her to feel unimportant. A mutual friend had referred her, so I called that person to get the information before my new client came to see me.

During Lindsey's session, I realized exactly why I kept forgetting her name: She believed that she was worthless and didn't deserve to be noticed! She'd spent her entire life creating experiences where she was never seen, recognized, or valued. Her unconscious voice spoke so loudly that even I had heeded it, responding by "not noticing" her name.

Parents and spouses may want to look at this principle closely. To do so, imagine putting on "spiritual eyeglasses" as you look at—and deal with—those you love. Here's an example: Kevin was convinced that his 14-year-old son, Jim, was irresponsible and lazy, and that he needed to learn better work habits. Jim continually confirmed his father's perception by acting out the behavior his father expected of him. One day, Kevin was out jogging with his wife, Jan, who observed traits in her husband that he saw in their son.

As Kevin began to complain about Jim's behavior, Jan wisely responded by asking, "In what ways is he teaching you something about yourself?" Kevin thought quietly and then began to have a different perception of the situation. He came home from his morning jog and retreated to a place where he could pray. He humbly asked God for the privilege of seeing Jim with divine eyes. Emotion quickly overwhelmed the frustrated father as he wept with a higher understanding of this great being, his son.

When he saw the gold within Jim, Kevin realized that his child was gifted with wisdom, intuition, and an amazing ability to love. This loving man began to give his son the greatest gift parents can give their children—seeing them the way that God does. As Jim became free to assume a different role in his family, his behavior improved, and so the gift of higher understanding touched the entire family.

Altering perceptions of spouses can prove just as powerful. Natalie had been married to Mike for four years, and they had an 18-month-old daughter. Natalie's father had abandoned her family during her teenage years. He had a pattern of dishonesty, and had betrayed her mother. Therefore, she was skeptical of men and held an unconscious belief that they're dishonest and can't be trusted—but she loved her husband.

Mike's mother had also experienced being abandoned by her father (Mike's grandfather), who was dishonest, and she carried a perception that men aren't to be trusted. As a direct result of his mother's perception and expectation, Mike grew up with the notion that no one could count on him. Consequently, he played out this role—even though he loved his wife.

As in most couples, Natalie and Mike had each attracted a mate with similar belief patterns. However, this particular pattern hurt their marriage. A requisite for a healthy relationship is trust, and their union was crumbling without it.

One evening, Natalie sat alone in her car and began praying. She didn't understand that she was holding a perception that could be contributing to Mike's actions. As she sobbed and expressed to God her desire to get a divorce, she heard these words clearly inside her mind: *If you could only see who he really is.*

Peace came over her, along with some understanding that there was more to her husband than she'd been able to see. She drove home, resolving to stay in her marriage, and she began to seek further insight into the truth about Mike—who he really was and who he could become.

They received years of counseling before they reconciled the individual issues that had ironically drawn them together and then pushed them apart. I worked with both of them for a while and was amazed by how each would identify a particular fault in the other, and then eventually come to see a similar pattern within him- or herself. Their hard work and diligence paid off; and they are currently in a happy, healthy relationship that's stable and fulfilling for both of them.

The greatest gift we can ever give to those we're trying to care for is to see something greater in them than they can believe themselves. This is the beginning of learning to love perfectly. However, it's increasingly difficult to do this when we're unwilling to see something spectacular within ourselves.

A blessing we can offer ourselves is to be willing to find something inside of us that's greater than the way we usually behave. Often, we wait to change until trials and hardships become so painful that they pull our very souls to heights we've never imagined. After the devastation on September 11, 2001, when terrorists attacked the World Trade Center in New York City and the Pentagon in Virginia, many Americans were surprised to learn how many remarkable people were living in their country. Then, in response to the tsunami disaster on December 26, 2004, charitable acts of citizens from all over the world literally rescued nations.

People often rise to heights of spirituality, selfless giving, and compassion after catastrophes such as these. While honoring the positive growth and change that was manifested in the world at these times, I believe that it isn't always necessary for such trauma to occur before we courageously rise up to display the potential of our characters.

We have the power to effect change, to free ourselves from the bondage of our daily trials, and to create peace and joy for our descendants, a gift that ultimately blesses our world. In order for this to happen, we must first believe in ourselves, and vow to transform our dysfunctional family patterns. We must trust that there's gold underneath all that plaster, and be willing to chip it away—piece by piece.

The Process

1. As you consider the light and dark qualities that exist within you, ask yourself these questions: *What character traits or behaviors do I most dislike in others, and why? What characteristics of others or myself stir emotion within me?*

2. Now consider these questions: *Who do I dislike the most and why? Who do I <u>not</u> want to be like, and why? In what ways am I similar to the person I <u>don't</u> want to resemble and/or the person I most dislike?* Take time to really think about this, and write down your answers.

3. When you've decided who you *don't* want to emulate, focus on someone you'd like to take after. Ask yourself: *Who do I want to be like, and why? Who do I admire the most, and what characteristics draw me to this person? In what ways am I similar to the person I want to resemble or the person I respect the most?*

4. Now focus on yourself for a moment. What is it about you that you're most afraid to see? Consider the answer to be a weakness, ready for you to confront, or a strength ready for you to own.

5. Next, ask: *Do I have strengths that may also be weak points? If so, what are they?* For example, if I'm a patient person, this becomes a liability if I "patiently" suppress my emotions and am dishonest about them, or I "patiently" withstand abuse when I should speak up.

6. Answer these questions: *What are the blessings that have come to me because of my failings? What gifts have I gained and what lessons have I learned from others' flaws?*

7. Finally, make a list of the things that you need to change within you to become more charitable toward yourself and others.

Chapter Five

Step 5:
Making a Spiritual Connection

5

Most religions and philosophies suggest that within each human body is a form of energy or intelligence that's greater and more powerful than we realize. Like a hand that fits inside a glove, this spirit lives within the flesh, animating us and directing our paths.

Today, perhaps more than ever, people want to understand more about spirituality. We want to know about our ability to tap in to a higher dimension of truth and light. In fact, such an endeavor is needed in order for families to heal. So many answers come and so many problems are resolved when we focus more on our spiritual identities than our worldly selves. It's our divine aspects that really shine.

For those who believe in God, it's not a stretch to assume that we're innately awesome. As His children, it only makes sense that we have some of His characteristics, which give us the potential to be extraordinary. Disbelieving our abilities or putting ourselves down means that we're condemning a child of God. I believe, as many do, that the Almighty has a purpose for each of us. Unless we're able to connect spiritually, listen and respond, and believe in our transcendent nature, we won't be able to fulfill that potential. The opportunity to discover it is given to all of us, and the choice to achieve is only ours to make.

When we move toward light (or knowledge and truth), we view ourselves more clearly—it's a natural consequence. As we do so, we become more aware of a fuller picture, which includes seeing both the positive and the negative characteristics that we possess. Much of this book discusses how to discover and cope with the darkness we experience within ourselves. In order to balance that, we need to know and access our light, too.

Ralph Waldo Emerson said, "What lies behind us and what lies before us are small matters compared to what lies within us." We can't become something great if we're not even aware that wonderful qualities exist within us. Knowing our spiritual identity is the key to changing our lives for the better, getting what we want, and creating more joy and happiness. And being humble enough to admit our shortcomings and heal them is the way we find that greatness.

The Hand and the Glove

Let's define two parts of our identity—the "hand" and the "glove." Let's say that the glove is the programmed human body that incorporates thought patterns, behaviors, and belief systems derived from our earthly experiences. It also includes genetic data, such as our height and the color of our hair, eyes, and skin. Gloves come in various sizes, colors, and fabrics, and they exist in many parts of the world. Each of them has one major purpose: to cover the hand. Without this, they lack life and purpose.

The hand can be compared to the human spirit, another part of our identity that fits inside the body. This part of ourselves may feel difficult to reach—after all, it's not physical in nature. But it's important for us to try to sense it. Without it, similar to an empty glove, we're basically useless, since it's enormously powerful.[1]

For most people, the spirit behind the human body is unseen and unfelt. Those who've experienced knowing this part of themselves usually testify that they connect to it through a process of "feeling," which is difficult to describe and is sometimes dismissed as crazy or unbelievable. Since so many individuals are trained to block out emotions, they have trouble sensing anything not in this realm. But those who are able to perceive it have reported that they feel love and peace, and often receive direction after connecting to their spirit selves. It opens their minds to new perceptions and inner knowledge that results in positive growth and change.

Science and Agency

As human beings, we have the power to choose our response in every situation, and our reactions are individual. In the gap between stimulus and response, which Stephen Covey discussed in the Foreword, we have the powerful opportunity to exercise agency—the ability to think, reason, and change. Nonetheless, we tend to naturally react according to instinct and prior conditioning, as though we were animals. But other creatures don't share our freedom of choice, intelligence, and capacity for transformation. Unless we allow our spirit selves to guide us—and we're committed to change—we typically struggle to alter our patterned behaviors.

Human responses are primarily based on conditioning. Where this begins is fascinating: While researching the origin of behavioral issues, I learned from Ranae Johnson, Ph.D., a researcher in the field of psychology and an expert in eye-movement therapy, that 75 to 90 percent of our emotional blocks—including our inborn (genetic) tendencies[2]—originate from our experiences within the womb. That figure tells us that most of our subconscious blocks (the emotions and fears that are preventing us from healing or simply holding up our progress) come from one of a few possibilities:

1. Emotional memories of our time in gestation

2. Any trauma or fear we experienced during the birthing process

3. Genetic inheritance, which means that we essentially brought them into the world with us

Dr. Johnson's research is backed up by other, new evidence. In 2005, *Biological Psychology* published a study conducted by Peter Hurd, Ph.D., indicating that a man's index finger length relative to his ring finger length can predict how inclined he is to be physically aggressive.[3]

This information is huge! It teaches us that only 10 to 30 percent of our core emotional blocks result from the experiences we face in life. These statistics validate our need to know about our conditioned and instinctual tendencies. When we're ignorant of them or simply don't want to alter our behavior, we limit our access to the mental agency we've been given. That's similar to running a computer system on a default setting: If we don't pick another option, we go through our lives according to our programmed responses.

To change, we must use our agency and make new choices. That's what this book is about—all the material in these pages is meant to help us distinguish our family patterns from our spiritual potential, giving us the power to make new decisions. It's a fact that we can't modify our behavior by running the same information through our brain that we had when we created the pattern. We can only move on when we have new data. The authority to do this belongs to us, and we increase our power as we become conscious, learning more about ourselves and growing into beings of light and truth.

Our spirit is loving and compassionate, as God is. It can step into the gap between stimulus and response and heal the natural, programmed part of us. It's better not to resist what dwells within us, but to seek its guidance—after all, it's easier to mold soft clay than hard rock. If God or a higher intelligence within us wants to make us into something great, wouldn't it be easier to soften our hearts and become pliable? Why wait for the world to fall down around us before we wake up to the notion that perhaps there's something better within us than we'd ever considered? We're meant to have joy and happiness, and in order to do so, we need to know ourselves better—both the spirit and the natural person.

The Intuitive Link

In a quiet place inside our minds and hearts rests a still, small voice—an inner-knowing genius. It's not the part of us that adds, subtracts, and multiplies, nor is it the logical mind that reasons and deducts. It's somewhat abstract and always accurate: our intuition. By listening to it, we can solve some of the most difficult problems that exist in our lives, and we can be guided to know simple things, too, such as where we placed our car keys and which direction we should go when we're lost.

I came to value my inner knowing as a child. When I was young, my mother would hold my hand and think about something, and within minutes, I'd start talking about whatever she'd thought. She found it fascinating. Today, there are all kinds of physical explanations for this phenomenon. Whether we call it psychic energy, extrasensory perception, or a spiritual connection, the art of listening to something speaking within—and then responding to it—is something I grew to value, and it's a powerful tool for me.

My mother valued her inner voice as well, and so did my grandmother. Wisely, my mom listened to this spirit to direct her life. It was common for her to throw all logic out the window if she had a "feeling" that she should do something. Once, when I was home from college for the summer, she came back from the grocery store with a large birthday cake. As far as I knew, it wasn't anyone's special day, so we were all curious as she unloaded the car and brought the cake inside.

"Whose birthday is it?" we shouted.

She replied, "I don't know, but I had a feeling that I should buy a cake, so I did."

Sure enough, within a day my mom discovered that a struggling, single mother living nearby was having a birthday and her young children wanted to give her a cake but weren't old enough to bake one. Voilà! Mom whipped the confection out of the fridge and was off to be of service to that family. For many years, they remembered the night she showed up with that birthday cake and left their mother filled with tears of gratitude. I learned to trust intuition more than logic because of many such experiences with my mother and grandmother.

Connecting Your Spirit with God's

You can talk to people every day who say that there's no such thing as the divine, intuition, or the spirit. If that's what you believe, then spirituality is far away and intuition won't be readily accessible. The divine and our inner knowing are only as accessible as we make them, and our spirit voices are only as loud as we allow them to be. At times, we all feel far removed from God or our higher identities. But just as we may want to stay close to someone who's been dear to us, but from whom we're separated at the moment, we know how to do it: We reach out. We listen, find ways to connect, and discover things to do for one another. The more often this happens—and the longer it continues—the deeper the affection. If much time passes without contact, the bond weakens or deteriorates.

I know there is a God, our Father in Heaven, who loves us and offers us the same opportunity to draw close to Him as would a loving friend. If we approach the relationship in that way, we find strength, love, growth, answers, knowledge, light, and truth. All this comes to us through what I call the spirit. It leaves us feeling worthy, loving others and ourselves more abundantly, and feeling prepared to serve and assist those in need.

Making the Right Connection

Many people pray and become frustrated when their prayers aren't answered in just the manner they expect. That's because they approach the process as if they were making a phone call and leaving a message on an answering machine—but they don't wait for a call back or further instruction. They don't know how to listen and respond to guidance that may help answer the prayer.

Most people believe that God has offered us a way to communicate, and that answers can come through prayer and meditation. But they forget that effective communication requires feedback, and prayer is a method of divine interaction. That means that someone puts forth information, and the receiver hears it and then sends back another message verifying the initial contact. Our intuitive connection is the method by which we receive the feedback. Without it, there's really no communication going on, and we have a more difficult time understanding the ways in which our prayers are being answered.

Elizabeth Barrett Browning wrote: "And every common bush [is] afire with God; but only he who sees, takes off his shoes." The critical question we can ask ourselves is: *Am I listening? Have I removed my shoes? And if I haven't, how can I go about it?*

To develop our intuitive connection, we must know what love feels like. Since God embodies this quality, a divine connection will feel positive, nonjudgmental, patient, and peaceful. If we aren't familiar with these attributes, we may not recognize the spirit. We don't want to wind up spatially disoriented, a condition that pilots experience when they're unknowingly headed in the wrong direction. In fact, they're usually convinced that they're on the right path. Without equipment and the wisdom to follow the flight signals (which will always provide the proper route, even when it seems incorrect), a pilot with this problem will crash. Love is the key to recognizing the spirit. We can use it as the sign to keep our inspiration clear and accurate.

Practice with Prayer

Practice makes perfect—that is, the more we listen and respond to the inner voice, the better we become at hearing it. We can access our intuition at any given time at any age. When my youngest son was six years old, he lost one of his first teeth. He was so thrilled that he carried it all over the house, showing every family member. Concerned that he might lose it, I suggested he place it in a Ziploc bag, so he did.

About an hour later, he told me that there was a hole in the bag and the tooth was no longer there. He showed me where he was when he noticed this, and we got down on our knees and started to search. The whole family crawled on the floor to help. After a long search, I finally gave up and offered him some money to make up for the fact that he couldn't leave his tooth for the fairy.

He was so sad that I also suggested he say a prayer in private and ask for an idea about where to look. Within minutes, he came to me and said, "Mom, open the dishwasher." I did, and lo and behold, there was his tooth, sitting in the soap container!

Prayer works at any age. There are no complicated prerequisites, only faith and desire. With these intentions in place, we can access an amazing communication tool, more powerful than any of today's technology. And using it can change our lives for the better—forever.

Since many of our family patterns are hidden and hard for us to see, listening to our intuition is vital to the healing process. What feels right for one person may not feel right for another. Since healing is individual, accessing personalized answers is essential. We need this kind of divine connection to mend our families, for without it, we won't be as effective.

Life Is Depressing Without a Connection

Our world has learned a lot about physical connections. In the past 150 years, new technology has included telephones, cell phones, computers, and the Internet. Today, these are all vital. The world economy and our individual lives don't seem to work without them. In fact, most Americans can't imagine being without computers, phones, and the Internet.

While seated on an airplane waiting to take off, I took note that a few hundred people, including me, were piled like sardines into the seats, not talking to one another. Many passengers were using cell phones and computers. I assumed that these people were sending text messages, checking e-mail, or leaving voice messages about our delayed flight. Few people were carrying on conversations with one another. I thought, *Why is everyone so attached to the Internet, the phone, and the computer?* As the idea came to me that everyone needs some kind of a connection, I also wondered, *Then why are so few of us connecting with those nearly touching us on the flight?*

Collectively speaking, many of us have become terrified of interpersonal communication. Today, most of our interactions with one another involve only superficial contact. We converse about topics that are generally physical in nature, such as what color our hair is, who won the World Series, or what the weather is like at the moment.

Not only do we limit ourselves to this type of trivial data, but we also aren't very honest about it. Studies show that most Americans lie in their casual conversations. In fact, researchers tell us that on average, 60 percent of the people we associate with will lie at least once during a ten-minute conversation, and most tell an average of two to three falsehoods.[4] People exaggerate the facts, create scenarios where they look good to others, and tell white lies to protect themselves. How's that for honest, healthy communication? Most of us don't even know how to do it.

Only about 5 percent of our discourse is personal and can be considered an honest expression of ourselves—our true thoughts and feelings.[5] This kind of exchange involves sharing information that could leave someone judging or criticizing us, and thus requires us to take a risk.

The problem is that most people need more personal or critical interaction in order to feel connected and loved. Sex is one way in which people can reach each other in a personal way, as it involves sharing, giving, and risking. But even intimacy has become very distant for many. No wonder we live in a world where people long to be connected—we usually want something we don't have.

Most of us desire to have someone in our world who understands us, cares for us, and is willing to listen to and respect our expression of ourselves. Everyone needs to be loved in this way. This is part of our nature and must be fulfilled in order for us to grow and develop a healthy sense of individual worth. Why do we limit this type of communication when it's vital for our growth and development? Often it's because we fear the judgment of others.

Casey—the Greatness of a Soul

My good friend Casey was born into an impoverished, abusive home where she didn't feel loved and accepted by her family. There was screaming, yelling, hitting, and fighting going on around her for most of her life. She was born with vision impairment that left her eyes crooked. As a young girl, she was teased by her peers and sexually molested by a family member.

I met Casey at church. She was shy and very likable, but she didn't come to meetings very often. Leaders from our church lovingly tried to help her from time to time, as she was in an abusive marriage, struggling with young children, and financially burdened. Sometimes their efforts were well received, but other times they weren't.

One afternoon I ran into Casey at the grocery store. She gave me a hug and said that she wouldn't be coming to church anymore. She explained that she didn't feel loved or accepted there, and she couldn't handle the pain. I was sad about her decision and wasn't sure what I could do to help. She wasn't a client, just a friend, so I didn't know how to approach what I believed to be one of her core issues.

About two years went by, and we had little or no contact until one afternoon when I got a call from another friend from church. She said that she'd stopped by to visit Casey and found her in a terrible emotional state—she was considering suicide. She asked if I could meet with this distressed woman right away.

Within 30 minutes, the two showed up at my door, and I had the opportunity to help Casey work through many core issues. Together, we uncovered the fact that deep down she was afraid of rejection. This fear left her feeling out of place and unable to connect with others, and she didn't believe in herself enough to be comfortable in a group. As an abused and molested child, she assumed that her girlhood hell was a reflection of her own worth. When she was associating with confident women at church, she felt small and insignificant. Rather than face the pain, she quit attending and blamed her inability to connect on the rude or unkind actions she identified in a few members.

I cried with Casey as I saw within her a little girl starving for a caring connection. She desperately needed friends and a place to fit in and be accepted, but she put up walls built out of a fear of rejection. The barriers cost her love, yet she subconsciously believed that they protected her from feeling the agony of worthlessness.

Ultimately, it doesn't matter what others think of us, but only what we believe to be true about ourselves. It's by knowing, loving, and accepting ourselves that we develop enough inner strength to be able to care for and support others. When we possess a healthy sense of self-worth, we tend to draw people into our lives who share our desire to love.

But what if we've felt bad about ourselves our whole lives and have no idea where to go to gain a better understanding of our individual value? What does someone like Casey do to feel connected? Countless people have existed in horrible circumstances for decades and never had anyone treat them as if they're worth something. This is where a belief in God and gaining a spiritual connection is vital.

In my session with Casey, I asked her to visualize Jesus Christ (because she's a Christian woman) standing in front of her. Then I suggested that she envision him handing her a mirror. I asked her to look inside and see a reflection of the greatness of her soul. She cried as she felt love for herself for the first time.

When we don't believe we're cherished, and instead feel bad about ourselves and suppress these emotions for a long time, we get depressed and overwhelmed, and sometimes entertain thoughts of suicide. Today, depression is widespread. Often, it's a sign that we need to see the good or divine within ourselves, or that we need to strengthen our spiritual connection. A visualization like the one I did with Casey can work for anyone, no matter what their religious preference. Simply adapt the mental picture to your own belief system. Anyone can envision a mirror descending from the powerful light of the sun, reflecting the divine self.

Because we may not know how to be spiritually connected—or even want to be—we may tend to shut off our emotions. That's because the spirit speaks to us through our intuition, and the process feels somewhat emotional. Consequently, we may be conflicted, wanting to heal our depression but unwilling to accept all aspects of ourselves. For a long time, Casey hurt so much that she didn't want to feel anything, including a spiritual connection.

Shutting off our emotional mechanisms and our higher selves can be costly. When we're depressed, we often have negative feelings, such as fear, sadness, guilt, shame, anger, frustration, and resentment. To get back in balance, we need to experience more love, forgiveness, and gratitude. Our spiritual bond can help us reach this balance almost instantly. True, it may not permanently take away the pain, since the unpleasant thoughts and beliefs usually need to be addressed. But a divine link can provide hope and relief.

Statistics tell us that people who believe in God are happier than people who don't.[6] Hope and peace come from having faith in the divine, and some problems are just too difficult to solve without such a connection.

Only God Really Knows

When King Louis XIV of France passed away, a grand state funeral was held in Notre-Dame Cathedral. The bishop of Paris stood in the pulpit to preach the eulogy and spoke just four words: "Only God is great."

There have been times in my life when I thought my problems weren't solvable. At these points, when I've approached my situation with prayer and meditation, new possibilities have surfaced through my spiritual connection. What was once impossible to figure out became reparable. When there's no other way, we can turn to God—often the only one great enough to resolve many of our troubles. As we listen, we can find direction.

One day a woman stopped me at a gas station and asked me how to get to Middleburg, Virginia, and I confidently gave her directions. I pulled out of the parking lot and headed down the road, only to realize that I'd given her inaccurate information. For the rest of the day, I was troubled about having wrongly advised her.

While many people may appear qualified to give us direction and intend to do us good, they might not know the right path for us. Luckily, a map exists somewhere inside us. Our spirit knows what's best for us, which way to go, and how to get there. By relying on our divine connection, we can be assured that we'll arrive at our eternal destinations quickly, and without many wrong turns.

Charting a New Course

When my oldest daughter turned eight, my father and I took her on a tour of East Coast historic sights. My father was a historian, and as we drove near Boston, he talked about the Pilgrims who'd come to Plymouth, Massachusetts. This community of religious settlers was originally assigned by the king of England to settle in what's now New York City, but their travel at sea set their ship off course by one degree. Consequently, the pilgrims landed at the tip of Cape Cod, rather than Long Island. The lead ship attempted to proceed southward through the Long Island Sound, but it was unsuccessful, as it kept hitting reefs that threatened to sink it. Word was sent to the king, and they were given permission to land in Plymouth instead.

As my father repeated this story, I thought of the lasting implications that resulted from a simple one-degree shift in direction, made hundreds of years ago. What seemed like a small change in course resulted in a long-lasting impact on the configuration of modern America.

The Dutch settled in what would become New York City, and their influence was different from the religious principles that guided the settlers to Plymouth.

So it is with us: The seemingly insignificant changes we make in ourselves and our relationships eventually affect the outcome of many lives. As parents, we have an obligation to our children and our world to chart new courses for ourselves that will lead to positive change.

As we work to forge ahead, no greater effort can be made than to become aware of our higher nature. This kind of effort has farther-reaching consequences than we're capable of truly foreseeing. We make a lasting difference in the lives of countless people when we're more conscious of our missions on this planet, but information about our purpose only becomes available when we know ourselves spiritually. Therefore, making a new path for future generations requires the willingness to look at ourselves honestly, including both the "hand" and the "glove."

Children are taught to follow authority. As their leaders, wouldn't it be fantastic if we could offer our kids more truth, answers, options, and positive changes? Perhaps we could alter the course of our family's future by modeling a spiritual journey. If we could break the chain of false teachings and offer them something other than our default programming, could we change the direction of the world?

The Path Home

I once knew a three-year-old named Alex. One early morning he crawled in bed with his mom, and the two had a blast snuggling. After a while, Alex said, "Mom, let's go home."

She laughed and answered, "Alex, we are at home."

"No, Mom, let's go home!" he insisted

It took her a minute to understand that he was talking about his heavenly dwelling. She was shocked when she realized what he meant, and quickly said, "No, Alex, I want to stay. Don't you like it here?"

"No, Mom, it's stupid here."

Although there might have been personal issues contributing to this little boy's feelings about living here on Earth, I still wonder how many other little ones feel that a lot of what goes on here is dumb. When we think about it, we realize that as adults, we often do foolish things for fairly unintelligent reasons. We pay lots of money to "lift" our brows (even though we teach our kids that their inner beauty is what counts); we work 16-hour days so that we can give more to our children (even though we end up giving them less of us) . . . you get the picture.

Becoming Like a Child

Many of today's spiritually gifted children wonder why we refuse to see the light around us and why we're so caught up in the games of this world that we're unable to connect to the divine purpose of this planet. Why are we more concerned about what others believe than what God thinks? Why are we so blocked energetically that we can't hear the whispering voices of ministering angels who are trying to guide and direct us? Children naturally possess a sense of knowing. They have an idea of who they are, why they're here, and where they came from—and even where they'll return—that most of us lose as we mature. They know where *home* is.

As parents, we must work to sustain this knowledge, honor their spirits, and support their destiny. In order to do this, however, we must know ourselves spiritually. We must, in a way, become more childlike.

My client Bryan has a four-year-old son named Sam who is very bright. Bryan was amazed by how well his son understood technology, and he also had an awareness about life that awed both his parents. One day, Sam was acting up and not minding his dad. After expending all the patience he had, Bryan firmly explained that the boy had better shape up. Sam looked his father straight in the eye and spoke calmly from his heart: "Dad, I'm stronger than you are." Bryan was shocked by these words, and by the child's confidence. This atypical statement was communicated honestly and with firmness.

Initially, my client started to battle with his son, explaining that he was the dad, so he was the strongest. But as he found himself saying this, he began to feel funny. In the back of his mind, he thought, *I wonder if he's right.* That night, Bryan found himself praying about his son. During his prayers he received a confirmation that Sam was right: The little boy *was* stronger, although his strength wasn't physical, but spiritual. He was a special kid, and he wanted his father to take note.

Generally speaking, our society expects good behavior from children, and we aren't always tolerant of unruly conduct—even if it's age appropriate. When kids act up, we tend to put them down or judge them. In the process, our youth can lose sight of their strength because they feel unworthy of it. As a result, they end up pulling the plug on their spiritual connections. In fact, this probably happened to us, too.

As time went by, Sam impressed his parents with an amazing ability to solve problems. A year later, his mother, Diane, was home alone with him, his little sister, and his newborn baby brother. Bryan had been out of town for several days when Diane, tired and overwhelmed, lost her patience with the children and sent Sam and his sister to their rooms.

Within five minutes, Sam calmly walked out and announced, "Mom, I prayed that you'd be able to be good. I also prayed for the rest of our family and asked that they'd be able to be good, including Dad. But I didn't have to ask for our baby to be good, because he's a baby, and he's always good. You should be feeling better any minute, Mom."

Sam has parents who are willing to acknowledge his worth, strength, and power. This is a good thing for him, and it's also a gift for the grown-ups. Throughout their years of parenting, Bryan and Diane will learn a lot. Their chances of helping this child develop into an emotionally stable adult are greater simply because they don't have to try to be stronger than he is, and they're willing to learn from him.

Sam's story isn't important just for parents; it's relevant for everyone. We all resemble this little boy, having strength beyond comprehension and the ability to outperform ourselves, and maybe even our parents. Tapping in to this strength often comes when we remember the child within. Chances are that this part of us remembers more about our spiritual strength than our adult self does.

Changing Through Charity

Abuse isn't affection, yet children who are mistreated have a hard time understanding that. No matter how you look at it (and despite popular music lyrics suggesting the contrary), real love doesn't hurt.

The real deal is charity—kindness, gentleness, and patience. It means accepting differences and the process of supporting someone even when they haven't handled something in the way we might have hoped. When we truly care, we don't take advantage of each other's weaknesses. We're receptive to other perspectives and perceptions, and we accept the best in each other. We're not critical, judgmental, or sarcastic. We're willing to be honest, and we take responsibility for our part of a problem.

The best place to learn this is in the home. But if you live in a dysfunctional family, understanding charity can be profoundly difficult. In these situations, love can sometimes be equated with abuse. Because the perpetrator—usually a parent or other close relative—is supposed to care (that's what families do, right?), most victims end up believing that something must be wrong with them. They suppose that they deserved everything because they're bad. They learn to hate themselves, and they fear uncovering their feelings of nothingness because their deep-seated wounds are so painful.

When a family member is abusive, the reality that love is absent in the home leads to dangerous beliefs that it can't be found at all—that affection isn't needed to make it through life. The only way to move beyond such feelings is to go above them and heal the soul with self-love based on the knowledge that we're all children of God.

This requires some work. Coming to know the divine attributes of a loving God requires us to separate the divine from our experience with our earthly parents, since we all tend to associate the Almighty with these early authority figures. Consequently, we attach our feelings and beliefs about our mom and dad with our spiritual perceptions. For example, if I believe that my father doesn't love me, that he abandoned me, and that he did so because I'm bad, I may think that God feels the same way. I may struggle throughout my life to understand how much He loves me.

God *is* love. He isn't fear or anger. And because He's all-knowing and loves us, He's also aware of our light and our goodness. Becoming aware of these positive qualities is getting to know yourself spiritually. When you feel bad about yourself, this is the perfect antidote. As you work past your fear and choose to let go of old ways, you'll show up in the world as magnificent, beautiful, and capable, which requires knowing the higher truth about yourself.

The Sufi poet Rumi wrote: "Out beyond the ideas of right doing and wrong doing, there is a field. I'll meet you there." The universe is an exceptional university, founded on agency, and the direction for the course of each of our lives may lie within a field that stretches beyond what we know. We can imagine that within that is God, present to counsel us at every moment as we exercise our right to choose for ourselves what we want and need in our lives.

At any given time we can decide to learn more about our spiritual identity, and doing so will help us to love and progress. Whenever we're overwhelmed with negative emotions or feel unloved, we can meditate and pray, closing our eyes, finding a place inside our hearts that's safe and beautiful, and then requesting help. We can ask to feel love in our lives again, or to be reminded of our own divinity. Afterward, with our inner knowing restored, we'll be better able to stay on track with our life's purpose and show charity and love toward others.

As you move forward in your healing work, remember this prayer, attributed to St. Francis of Assisi:

> *Where there is hatred, let me sow love;*
> *where there is injury, pardon;*
> *where there is doubt, faith;*
> *where there is despair, hope;*
> *where there is darkness, light;*
> *where there is sadness, joy.*

> *Grant that I may not so much seek*
> *to be consoled as to console;*
> *to be understood, as to understand;*
> *to be loved, as to love;*
> *for it is in giving that we receive;*
> *it is in pardoning that we are pardoned;*
> *and it is in dying that we are born to Eternal Life.*

May God bless you on your eternal path to wholeness.

The Process

1. Because our relationship with our parents can color our perception of God, try to separate the traits that belong to your mom and dad from the true and loving attributes that belong to the divine. To do so, make a list of fears or judgments you have about God. Then go over your list and see if your ideas are really your perception of one or both of your parents.

2. As you consider that you might have a higher self or spiritual identity, ponder the answers to these questions:

   - How can I establish an individual and intimate relationship with God?

   - How can I improve the relationship I already have with God?

   - How can I feel God's love for me daily?

   - How can I forgive myself so that I can feel God's love for me?

   - How can I love and support myself as God does?

   - What messages do I send to others that dishonestly represent my true identity?

   - How does my dishonesty about my worthiness stop others from feeling valued?

- What lies do I tell myself that keep me from seeing the truth about me?

- How do I prevent God or my higher self from revealing the truth to me about who I really am?

3. Write a private letter to God. Pour out your heart, asking that you might be guided and blessed as you proceed to heal.

4. Pray and meditate. Ask to have a greater knowledge of your divine worth.

CONCLUSION

What to Expect as You Heal

*T*his book came to be after years of my working on myself, and after gaining this "personal" education (which included my family's issues), I was able to see and understand so many other people. I learned that our guide to truth and higher intelligence always comes from within. External information only prompts us to remember what we somehow already knew. Truth is eternal and unbendable, and it feels good to all who grasp it, if only for a time. Seeking after it is how we mend our lives, since it's our search for it that allows us to know and love ourselves.

My intention in writing is to help others heal. My self-exploration led me to realize that most of us don't know ourselves—that is, what we think and feel and why. A close friend said to me that we live in a world of plastic feelings, ones that aren't real. Most of us don't know our true emotions. We pretend that we don't have them, or we aren't honest about them. Similar to an iceberg, there's a lot of substance below the surface that explains the development and outcome of our lives.

While it may seem easier to ignore or deny the powerful weight of the ice below the water, in reality, it's much harder to live our lives unconsciously, believing it isn't there. When we know ourselves, however, we can change. When we overcome our fear of knowing, we can be happy; and when we begin to heal, we finally begin getting the love we need. Isn't that what we ultimately want most—to love and be loved?

Hands-On Learning

We have a tremendous opportunity to grow while we live in this universe. We can learn in many different ways, but the best method is hands-on. Did you understand (and remember) more as a child when you learned about a geographical location in the classroom, or when you traveled there on a field trip? In this life, we not only have the opportunity to find out about feelings, we get to experience them, and there are so many. If we suppress our pain, we don't allow ourselves to grow because of it. It's sad when we let valuable opportunities to progress slip through our fingers.

We are, in fact, co-creators of our world. While many believe that God has a hand in all things, we must consider that we also contribute to the outcomes of our lives. It's easy to blame the universe and other people when things don't go our way. But as a co-creator, we have the power and authority to chart a healthy, balanced, and loving life. This is the agency we've been divinely given.

Conclusion

The Evolution of Healing

Healing is an evolution. I've had frustrated friends wonder why certain issues keep surfacing and why just one counseling session doesn't fix everything, but they've missed the point of living and gaining knowledge. Life is a university, and becoming conscious is the laboratory where we can iron out all the confusion that exists within us—and learn! In the process, we're perfected. Some people assume that perfection is an action word, but it's really a *being* word. As we gain this ideal, we become more educated. What better wisdom can we acquire than to grow within ourselves, and subsequently, *into* ourselves.

When our perception has changed inside, our view of the world is altered, too—that's what shifting is. We naturally do this when we make an adjustment in our subconscious mind. This process of transformation occurs inside of us and around us because we shifted our consciousness. Since change often seems scary, the process can feel frightening. I've had clients say that they feel as if they're dying, and the truth is that a part of them *is* passing way. We evolve when we grow: Parts of us die off (such as old ideas and behaviors), making room for new growth, ideas, and ways of being.

Staying Grounded During Transformation

Often, we want to change our outer world so that we can be happy. If our inner landscape is modified first, then often the external one doesn't need to be altered so drastically for us to get what we want and need. While transforming, I've had clients fear that they need to file for divorce, cut off a relationship, quit a job, or move. But it's wise to stay grounded and balanced during the shifting process. This isn't a good time to make permanent decisions about our physical lives, such as moving, quitting work, or ending a marriage. Instead, we should nurture ourselves by eating healthy foods and exercising appropriately.

I recommend that you sit tight with any big changes until you feel that you've moved on from your processing. Typically, my clients go through a period of anywhere from a day to a week and sometimes even longer, where the world outside of them looks and feels different. After shifting, there may be a need to readjust your life in a profound way, perhaps by getting a new job, moving, or ending a relationship. I like to remind people to make absolutely certain that an abrupt switch is what they really need—and is for the best—before proceeding.

It's Okay to Cry

It's important to know that crying is the body's natural way of releasing pent-up emotions and stress. When working on personal and family issues, it's common to go through periods of time when we feel like weeping, since that's part of the way we release and heal. Healing can be quick, but not so fast that we don't have time to feel.

There's pain involved as we let go of the sad and bring in the glad. In fact, I'm usually more concerned about people who say that they never, ever cry, than people who say that they do so often. However, excessive tears can be a sign that something is wrong and you may need

help. If you're crying too much and you're concerned about it, check with a qualified health professional. Also, if you feel at any time that you may be suffering from depression or need medical attention for any other reason, contact a qualified health-care provider immediately. Some self-help processes require professional assistance for those with certain needs or conditions.

Feel the Joy

The ultimate objective is for men and women to experience joy. While many of us feel that our childhoods were lacking, all of us have an opportunity to create something more in the family we build later in life. This is something I've learned and something I've done. Despite our natural human tendencies to step back into the old patterns we learned from our heritage, we *can* transform—and that change can be easier if we're willing to go through the process of healing.

AFTERWORD

One Last Look at the Past

*A*s you move on, take the opportunity to consider the title of this book: *Healing Your Family History.* The ideas in the title—and certainly the book itself—have asked you to look at your past. You know that *you* want to heal, but do your ancestors want or need you to change and progress? If, like me, you believe in life after death, it's possible that they do. I had to seriously consider this concept after having an unusual experience late one cold winter night.

The Cowboy in My Mind

It was approaching 1 A.M., and my family had gone to bed. Enjoying a few quiet moments to myself, I curled up in front of a hot fire that my husband had built in our wood-burning stove. Almost baking from the heat, I began to drift off to sleep. In this half-awake state, I became aware of a strange man standing above me, wearing a cowboy hat and smiling down at me. He seemed to care about me a lot. Seeing him instantly woke me, and

I sat up quickly and looked around to make sure I was alone. I felt a bit scared as I thought, *I couldn't possibly be dreaming, could I?* No one was in the room, so I quickly dismissed the experience, hurried off to bed, and fell sound asleep.

The next day, my father called to chat. We talked about kids and family—all the usual stuff. Toward the end of our conversation, I told him about my odd experience in front of the fire. My father responded, "Well, your great-great grandfather Jim was a cowboy."

As a professional genealogist, my father boasted an incredible knowledge of our family's history. He'd authored five or more novels about our ancestors, which were bound and placed in genealogical libraries. Copies were in my home, too, but because of my lack of interest in such things, I'm sad to say that I'd only opened a couple of them. If anyone could tell stories about my ancestors, it was my dad—and certainly not me.

I felt a lump developing in my throat as my father talked. He told me that at a young age, Jim had moved with his parents to southern Texas. On the way there, his parents became ill, and they were all quarantined on an island in the Gulf of Mexico. They died there, leaving my great-great-grandfather orphaned. A messenger got word to a family member residing in Texas, who traveled to the island, claimed the young boy, and subsequently raised him.

This story was heartbreaking. I had two young sons of my own, so the thought of my great-great-grandpa experiencing abandonment as a child was terribly sad. I wanted to know more, so Dad went on.

As a teenager, Jim turned into a wild young man. With a rebellious attitude, he left home and rode off to

become a cowboy. As was common at the time, guns and shooting were part of his daily life. He lived his days with reckless abandonment and began to run into trouble with the law. At one point, he was arrested and jailed for murder, charged with killing a Mexican man. At some point, Jim ran off with my great-great grandmother Lucy. The kind, petite, pretty daughter of a well-to-do couple, she lovingly cared for her husband, and they had a family of 16 children.

Wow! What an extraordinary story, I thought.

While my dad was talking, I was quietly wishing that I could see a picture of this ancestor. As he finished, my father said, "Becky, you have a photo of him in one of my books." After we hung up, I ran to the bookshelf by the piano in the living room and searched through every page of that volume until I found the right image. I was speechless when I realized that the man in the photo— my great-great-grandfather Jim—was indeed the man I'd seen the night before.

I was anxious and excited to learn more. Lucky for me, the entire history was recorded and sitting at my fingertips. As I read, I found that Jim had lived life like a character in a John Wayne western. He was a strong and handsome cowboy who rode the dangerous Chisholm Trail in Texas. My father wrote: "Anything and everything went up the trail in 1871, and anything and everything went on. There was cowboy attitude and competition, cultural differences and prejudices, and conflicts which were settled quickly and permanently with the convenient, ever-present six-shooter."

My great-grandmother wrote in her autobiography that Grandpa Jim "had a mean streak, and was supposed to have killed a Mexican who knew too much about something. He was killed cold blooded, according to what was told me."

What does this mean? I wondered. As a teacher in the field of psychology, I thought of the many studies that connect the mind to the body and the research explaining that our physical selves may contain parts of the emotional memories and thought processes of our ancestors.

I studied more about Jim's life, thought about what his feelings would have been, and began to piece together what I supposed was his emotional profile. Because I'd conducted hundreds of private therapy sessions by the time I had this experience, I was capable and qualified to make certain assumptions. With this information, I started reconstructing a portion of my family history— not the physical relationships, but a part of the emotional map that may have led my relatives to behave and believe—and thus, create—their lives in certain ways.

Deep inside Grandpa Jim's tough exterior was probably a young boy who was hurt, afraid, and lonely. His fears may have prevented him from fostering loving relationships and moving forward in a successful way. Jim was like many of us today: Unintentionally, our pain from the past may lead us to make choices that can cause suffering for others.

When we've been wronged by our ancestors, the chances are that a deep look into their lives may lead us to understand that they did the best they could with what they knew and understood at the time. It makes it easier to forgive and forget when we can empathize with their circumstances and understand their history. Doing so helps us turn our hearts toward them, rather than away, which we must do if we're to heal our family history.

The Path to Love

All techniques, programs, theories, and religious teachings succeed and thrive when they're founded on loving principles. Processes that teach principles contrary to this will fail over time. Likewise, families that participate in thought processes and subsequent behaviors that are founded in fear, withdraw love from the group. In time, these groups experience accelerated dysfunction. Whether or not we like the people in our families, learning to care for them is essential to understanding how to cherish ourselves. Since we're part of these individuals, judging, hating, fearing, or disowning them means doing those things to ourselves.

My search to know my great-great-grandfather—and thus better understand myself—led me to foster a greater love for my family. I never met that cowboy in the flesh, only in my mind's eye that winter night, but I can say that I have a greater devotion to my family after becoming more aware of his struggles as a child. My heart is full of compassion as I hear the story of his life.

I know that others loved Grandpa Jim, despite his dysfunction; my dad is one, and my grandmother is another. They managed to get past the tough exterior and love the crazy old man he became. Children, in particular, naturally adore their parents. It isn't until we grow older that we start judging and disowning them. That's the great thing about families: Despite the rough times and the pain, we have a natural desire to reach out to each other. When we can do so, we can heal. When we can't, we often wind up feeling unloved, unsupported, rejected, or abandoned. Then we set ourselves up to pass our fears and pain along to our children.

How many of us feel these terrible things? How many of us hand them down to our kids? Considering the massive dysfunction of our world, I would assume that lots of us experience these emotions deep down, even if we don't want to admit it. How important is it for us to identify these underlying fears and gain our sense of personal worthiness and positive connection to our families? This process is essential in order for our world to heal and change.

To this day, I'm not exactly sure why I saw Jim's face in my mind that cold winter night—perhaps the experience was meant to teach me something new about my ancestors and myself. From a spiritual standpoint, I'd like to believe that if there is life after death, Jim has a personal interest in me and was smiling at me because he loves me. Perhaps, wherever he is, he has a special desire to heal his family.

ACKNOWLEDGMENTS

I'm grateful for my children, who gave up time that would have been ours together had I not been writing this book. Likewise, I'm grateful to my husband, Shane, for picking up the pieces at home so that I could lock myself away in my home office to finish this project. We've been through a lot together, and without him, I wouldn't be me, and I couldn't have written this book.

The way I see the world, the healing I've processed, and who I've become is the result of the love of many. I couldn't list them all. However, I will acknowledge a few key figures who assisted me in creating, developing, and producing this project.

First, this book would not be in existence without the amazing editorial skills of Stephanie Gunning and Janna DeVore. Stephanie held my hand through the process of organizing and creating the book. Janna rescued me in the end and pulled the book together with her outstanding editorial talents, making the final revisions. To both, I am ever so grateful.

Next, and just as important, I'm grateful to Stephen Covey for breaking his "no Foreword" policy and strongly advocating the development of this project. His endorsement made possibilities available that otherwise wouldn't be. Thank you, Dr. Covey.

And thank you to my other great mentors who have endorsed this work: James Jones, Ph.D.; Christiane Northrup, M.D.; and Marie Osmond.

Thanks must also go to Stephany Evans of the Imprint Agency for agreeing to represent me and coordinate the sale of this book.

To all of the kind employees at Hay House, I'm pleased to be part of the team, and I'm grateful to Jill Kramer for her personal excitement and commitment to this title.

I'm thankful to my many clients who have trusted me, shared, and listened. Our teachers are our students, and our students are our teachers. Thank you for allowing me to learn from you.

I'm grateful to some key friends, particularly Mariellen Tuckett, who walked, talked, and encouraged my progress. Connie Boucher gave me physical support, encouraged me with love, and listened. Janine See's support kept me on track. And thanks to friends Lisa Bergman and Lori Wynn for reading and advice. I'm also grateful to Emily Carbone, a family friend and editor who agreed, at the last minute, to do a review.

My mother, Nancy Linder, has always been my best friend. My kids joke about the many times that Grandmother will call in one day. If it weren't for my mom's never-ending love and support of me, I wouldn't have completed this project.

Likewise, I'm thankful to my father, Bill R. Linder, for his love of family-history work and for sharing his gift of writing.

I am grateful to be in *The Club* (years ago, my sister and I decided we'd call our family *The Club*). As the oldest of five, I was the first sibling member. Every day I'm grateful for the love and influence of *The Club*. Thank you for everything, *Pretty Sisters*, Martha Montagnoli and Callie Steuer, and extraordinary brothers Richard and Robert Linder.

ENDNOTES

Foreword

1. Viktor Frankl, *Man's Search for Meaning* (New York: Buccaneer Books, 1959).

Introduction

1. Christiane Northrup, *Mother-Daughter Wisdom: Creating a Legacy of Physical and Emotional Health* (New York: Bantam Books, 2005), 3.

2. These statistics and more facts about the powerful role fathers play in the lives of children can be found in this book by Jeffery M. Leving, with Kenneth A. Dachman, Ph.D.: *Fathers' Rights: Hard Hitting and Fair Advice for Every Father Involved in a Custody Dispute* (New York: Basic Books, 1997), 46.

3. Northrup, *Mother-Daughter Wisdom*, 3.

4. Steven Pinker, *The Blank Slate: The Modern Denial of Human Nature* (New York: Viking, 2002).

5. Candace B. Pert, *Molecules of Emotion: Why You Feel the Way You Feel* (New York: Scribner, 1997).

6. Nancy L. Segal, *Entwined Lives: Twins and What They Tell Us about Human Behavior* (New York: Dutton Books, 1999).

Chapter One

1. Harville Hendrix, *Getting the Love You Want: A Guide for Couples,* (New York: Henry Holt, 1988), 9.

Chapter Two

1. Max Lucado, *If Only I Had a Green Nose* (Wheaton, Ill.: Crossway Books, 2002).

2. See David Popenoe, Debunking Divorce Myths (New Brunswick, N. J.: The National Marriage Project at Rutgers University, 2002), http://health.discovery.com/centers/loverelationships/articles/divorce.html; see also Popenoe, *Life without Father: Compelling New Evidence That Fatherhood and Marriage Are Indispensable for the Good of Children and Society* (New York: Martin Kessler Books, 1996).

Chapter Three

1. Kathryn Black, *Mothering without a Map: The Search for the Good Mother Within* (New York: Viking, 2004).

2. Bernie S. Siegel, *Love, Medicine & Miracles: Lessons Learned about Self-Healing from a Surgeon's Experience with Exceptional Patients* (New York: Harper & Row, 1986).

Chapter Four

1. Deepak Chopra, *Ageless Body, Timeless Mind: The Quantum Alternative to Growing Old* (New York: Three Rivers Press, 1993), 3.

2. Debbie Ford, *The Dark Side of the Light Chasers: Reclaiming Your Power, Creativity, Brilliance, and Dreams* (New York: Riverhead Books, 1998), 11–22.

3. James J. Jones, *"Let's Fix the Kids!": A Parenting Resource Manual,* 6th ed. (J. J. Jones, 1997).

4. Bunji Tozawa and Norman Bodek, *The Idea Generator: Quick and Easy Kaizen* (Vancouver, Wash.: PCS Press, 2001).

5. Norman Bodek, "Mistakes," *Strategos Lean Briefing* (Newsletter of Lean Manufacturing & Factory Science), July 28, 2003; see also http://www.strategosinc.com/briefs18.htm

Endnotes

6. See Thomas R. Lee, Wesley R. Burr, Ivan F. Beutler, Floyd W. Yorgason, Brent H. Harker and Joseph A. Olson, "The Family Profile II: A Self-Scored Brief Family Assessment Tool," *Psychological Reports* 81, no. 2 (1997): 467–77.

Chapter Five

1. See Boyd K. Packer, *Teach Ye Diligently* (Salt Lake City, Utah: Deseret Book, 1975), 273–76, for more on the glove/hand analogy.

2. Ranae Johnson, Ph.D., is the founder of The Rapid Eye Institute and the creator of Rapid Eye Technology (RET). She is an expert in healing blocks that originate from birth. More information about Dr. Johnson and her research can be found on her Website, **www.rapideyetechnology.com** or by reviewing education materials published by The Rapid Eye Institute, Salem, Oregon, 509–399–1181.

3. Peter Hurd and Allison A. Bailey, "Finger Length Ratio (2D:4D) Correlates with Physical Aggression in Men but Not in Women," *Biological Psychology* 68, no. 3 (March 2005): 215–22.

4. See Robert S. Feldman, J. A. Forrest, and B. R. Happ "Self-Presentation and Verbal Deception: Do Self-Presenters Lie More?" *Basic and Applied Social Psychology* 24 (June 2002):163–70.

5. Statistics presented by Douglas E. Brinley, Ph.D., "Strengthening Your Marriage and Family," Brigham Young University Campus Education Week seminar, August 2005.

6. This and similar facts about happy people can be found in David G. Myers, "The Funds, Friends, and Faith of Happy People," *American Psychologist* 55, no. 1 (January 2000): 56–67.

ABOUT THE AUTHOR

Rebecca Linder Hintze is an emotional wellness coach. A former broadcast journalist, she frequently lectures and leads workshops in cities around the world on topics such as Healing Your Family History, Strengthening Relationships, and Resolving Marital Conflict. Rebecca is the author of a successful weekly newsletter called *Weekly Wisdom*, published as a public service online and in print. She's also the author of a healing workbook entitled *It's Time to Dance*.

Rebecca is a graduate of Brigham Young University. She has pursued additional private course work in neuro-linguistic programming, rapid-eye-movement therapy, visual-blueprint analysis, emotional release therapy, muscle response testing, and holistic health medicine. In 2005, she cofounded *Pretty Sisters,* a worldwide society for girls of all ages (for more information, see **www.pretty sisters.com**). She's happily married to Shane Hintze, and together they have four children. For more information, visit **www.rebeccahintze.com**.

Notes

Notes

Notes

Notes

Notes

Notes

Notes

Notes

Notes

Notes

We hope you enjoyed this Hay House book.
If you'd like to receive a free catalog featuring additional
Hay House books and products, or if you'd like information
about the Hay Foundation, please contact:

Hay House, Inc.
P.O. Box 5100
Carlsbad, CA 92018-5100

**(760) 431-7695 or (800) 654-5126
(760) 431-6948 (fax) or (800) 650-5115 (fax)
www.hayhouse.com® • www.hayfoundation.org**

Published and distributed in Australia by: Hay House
Australia Pty. Ltd. • 18/36 Ralph St. • Alexandria NSW 2015
Phone: 612-9669-4299 • *Fax:* 612-9669-4144 • www.hayhouse.com.au

Published and distributed in the United Kingdom by:
Hay House UK, Ltd. • 292B Kensal Rd., London W10 5BE
Phone: 44-20-8962-1230 • *Fax:* 44-20-8962-1239 • www.hayhouse.co.uk

Published and distributed in the Republic of South Africa by:
Hay House SA (Pty), Ltd., P.O. Box 990, Witkoppen 2068
Phone/Fax: 27-11-706-6612 • orders@psdprom.co.za

Published in India by: Hay House Publications (India) Pvt. Ltd.,
Muskaan Complex, Plot No. 3, B-2, Vasant Kunj, New Delhi 110 070
Phone: 91-11-4176-1620 • *Fax:* 91-11-4176-1630
www.hayhouseindia.co.in

Distributed in Canada by: Raincoast • 9050 Shaughnessy St.,
Vancouver, B.C. V6P 6E5 • *Phone:* (604) 323-7100
Fax: (604) 323-2600 • www.raincoast.com

Tune in to **HayHouseRadio.com**® for the best in inspirational
talk radio featuring top Hay House authors! And, sign up via
the Hay House USA Website to receive the Hay House online
newsletter and stay informed about what's going on with your
favorite authors. You'll receive bimonthly announcements
about: Discounts and Offers, Special Events, Product Highlights,
Free Excerpts, Giveaways, and more!
www.hayhouse.com®